To Susa...
With much love,
Jessie

GIFT IN MY ARMS

Thoughts for New Mothers

Lois Walfrid Johnson

AUGSBURG Publishing House
Minneapolis, Minnesota

To Gail,
first to teach me
the joy of motherhood

Contents

Preface

In the joy-filled minute of birth or in that sunlit moment when you see the child you have chosen to adopt, you receive God's gift in your arms. You become a mother.

Yet none of us are instant mothers. Throughout the many years of our lives, we are always in the process of becoming.

That process, like the bursting of tulips through the earth, offers endless variety. First we see the spear reaching upward, then the leaf, the bud, and at last, the full-blown flower. As in the unfolding process of motherhood, each stage has a beauty of its own.

For no two women will the years be exactly the same. Each of us encounters different circumstances. Each of us reacts in a variety of ways. As our children are individuals, so are we. Yet we can hope our motherhood will develop in us the beauty of unfolding petals, revealing our growth in understanding and wisdom, in hope, in faith, and most of all in love.

In many ways the processes of becoming a mother

and of writing a book are similar. My thanks to those who have supported me in prayer during these times. My appreciation, also, to those who have influenced my attitudes toward motherhood or who have helped in writing this book: my husband and our three children, my parents, my mother-in-law, Hope and Leighton Erickson and their daughter Iantha, Catharine Brandt, Dr. Bruce Cameron, Dr. Mark Hillmer and his daughter Cathy, Ron and Lyn Klug, and Margaret Schilling.

Some sections of this book are written especially for biological mothers, others for adoptive ones. Most are meant for both. Three prayers are intended to be read by the mother and father together.

In your own process of becoming, may you know the beauty of God's growth. As you are a blessing to the child in your arms, may that gift be a blessing to you.

YOUR GIFT TO ME

Lord, I sense your presence
through the miracle of my child.
My child, yes—
but your gift to me.
In this intertwining of joy and responsibility
I consecrate myself
to the calling of becoming a mother.
I ask for your wisdom,
your understanding,
your ability to help me grow.
Without you the years loom too large;
with you I reach out in confidence,
accepting whatever moments lie ahead
for me
and for this gift in my arms.

1

Child in my arms

Moments after our third child was born, a nurse laid him within the circle of my arms. My hands tightened around him, eager, unbelieving, receiving this moment as the gift it was.

His skin was red, his earlobes covered with fine, blond fuzz. His two-inch-long hair stood out in every direction. Yet as I unwrapped the flannel blanket, I discovered each tiny finger was there, each tiny toe.

And all I could say was, "Hi, honey! You're a nice one."

The sexual experience during which a seed is implanted is a time of heightened emotion. So, too, is the time when the nourished seed emerges as a newborn. We stand on emotional tiptoe. Yet our feelings surrounding the birth are of greater variety and range out over a longer period of time—days and even months.

We watch our child's birth in the mirror, listening for the voice that says, "It's a boy!" or "It's a girl!"

In the moment which seems to last forever we wait for the cry—hearty, frantic, piercing.

We ask, "Is my baby okay?"

Then we relax, blanketed by exhaustion, satisfied for the moment that our child is all right.

Later we will seek out details. We will be reassured when the doctor says everything is normal. For now, we are delighted to see the look in the eyes of our husband as he first sees his child. For now, we are content to watch a small chest move up and down, in and out. There is life!

We are content to see tiny feet we have known before only through movements in our abdomen or as protruding kicks. To see slender fingers, clenched tight. To watch our child, eyes squeezed shut, crying without tears. For there God is acting, creating each muscle, developing each tear duct.

Yes, we can seek out details later. During this moment, we feel relief that our time of waiting is over. The unknowns of birth are behind us. In their place, we welcome the love of our husband. We experience the warm glow of his "I'm so glad you're all right."

If we were fortunate enough to have him in the labor and delivery rooms, we know the satisfaction of shared memories. We know the gentleness of his touch as he rubbed our back. We know the emotional support that flowed into us as he held our hand during contractions. We sensed, "I know what to do because he's here with me."

Best of all, we shared the moment when a tiny head and a small body emerged. We shared that first instant of seeing our child. And as we looked at one another we thought, "Out of all the countless possibilities, this is *our* miracle. Not put together at random—unique, yet possessing some of both of us."

If we were not together during the moment of birth, the time for that togetherness is now. To catch up on all that happened in those minutes when we were separated. To see tears in the eyes of our husband, perhaps for the first time in our marriage. To see him grin sheepishly as he admits, "That's the second time. I couldn't see very well when I held our baby."

Or, if our husband keeps his emotion hidden, to hear the gruffness in his voice. To hear him clear his throat. To know by the way he kisses us that the miracle dwells within.

And then we try to sleep. Too excited at first, we gradually drift off. We wake. We long for a shower. We breathe a prayer, "Thanks, Lord, for this time when I can rest and let others wait on me."

Soon the hours blur together, highlighted by each opportunity to hold our newborn, by the pleasure of a small mouth against our breast, a small head resting on our arm.

And as we nestle our infant's body into the softness of our own, we wonder, "God, is this how you love me—as though you were taking care of each detail of my life, with your arms around me?"

We remember the prophecy: "Behold, a young woman shall conceive and bear a son, and shall call his name Immanuel"—God with us (Isa. 7:14).

We remember the fulfillment: "And the Word became flesh and dwelt among us, full of grace and truth" (John 1:14).

Another Child. Another time. Another miracle.

Among us.

And the miracle continues as we receive your love in the form of your Child, as we claim the promise, "But to all who received him, who believed in his name, he gave power to become children of God" (John 1:12).

We trust, God, receiving the rest of your promise:

"All those who believe this are reborn!—not a physical rebirth resulting from human passion or plan—but from the will of God" (John 1:13 LB).

Birth and rebirth.

We receive, God. We receive.

Your love reaches me, God,
in this moment when I receive my gift.
Even as your Son became flesh
and dwelt among us,
so has this, my child,
become a new revelation of your creation.

Thank you for that awesome instant
when the whole earth seemed to pause,
waiting with me for that first hearty cry.
Thank you for smooth cheeks, a fuzzy head,
the pulsing of a tiny chest.
Thank you for your care of me,
your care of my child,
and your care in sending YOUR Child to us.
I accept all of your gifts.
Thank you, God.
Thank you.

2

Celebration of life

In the hours following our child's birth we wonder, "Do the relatives know? What about our friends?"

If we left children at home, we ask, "How are they doing? What did they say?"

With each rose or carnation, with each well-wishing card, with each gaily wrapped gift, we celebrate. With each smile, with each visitor, with each walk down the hall to view our newborn in the nursery, we celebrate.

"I think she looks like you. No, more like your husband."

"He has your father's nose."

"What a good baby she's going to be. Look at the way she sleeps."

We smile, still weak enough to crave getting back to bed, yet wanting to hear their congratulations.

Yes, we celebrate.

If sibling visitor privileges are allowed, our husband brings the child or children we left at home. It seems years since we felt their arms around our neck. Already they have grown. Our husband holds them up to the nursery window so they, too, can view the new arrival while we snap pictures of their reactions.

Yes, we celebrate. With friends, with relatives, with our husband.

"You know, I hate to go home when you aren't there," he says. Or "I'll be glad when we can be together nights again."

The laughter between us warms our entire being. It's good to be missed, we realize.

Together we make the final decision, naming our child.

We celebrate.

With newly opened eyes we understand how Mary and Elizabeth felt on that long-ago day as they saw one another. When Elizabeth heard Mary's greeting, she was filled with the Holy Spirit and cried out:

> "Blessed are you among women, and blessed is your child! What an honor it is to have the mother of my Lord come to see me! Why, as soon as your greeting reached my ears, the child within me jumped for joy! Oh, how happy is the woman who believes in God, for he does make his promises to her come true!"

We understand, too, why Mary answered:

> "My heart is overflowing with praise of my Lord, my soul is full of joy in God my Savior. For he has deigned to notice me, his humble servant and, after this, all the people who ever shall be will call me the happiest of women! The one who can do all things has done great things for me—oh, holy is his Name! Truly, his mercy rests on those who fear him in every generation" (Luke 1:42-50 Phillips).

Yes, we celebrate. With our friends, our relatives, our children, our husband.

We celebrate.

We've celebrated before, Lord—
my husband and I—
each moment the earth was touched by spring,
each night the moon formed lacework in the trees,
each time we walked together arm in arm.
But this is different, even better,
for together we sense our oneness
in this all-encompassing joy.

Our love created this sleeping infant, Lord,
and your power gave the breath of growth and life.
So together we celebrate that love!
We celebrate the uniqueness of our newborn child!
We celebrate the beauty of your creation!
We celebrate, Lord. We praise you
in the wonder of your work.

3

Lead me, Shepherd, lead me

"I felt joy about my son the moment I saw him," said one new mother. "Yet since then I've learned I was fortunate. Other women have mentioned they weren't able to get excited about their infant right away."

If we're one of those with a delayed reaction, it's easy to wonder, "Why do I feel a bit detached about my baby?"

Perhaps all we need is time to become acquainted. As a mother of four remarked, "At first I was just relieved it was all over. I was thankful the baby was okay. But I guess I'm not the kind who gushes over anyone. With each of my children, I felt the need to grow in a relationship, as I would with any friend."

But sometimes the circumstances surrounding birth interfere not only with our feelings of joy but also with our growth in love. We may think of Christ's comparison of the joy of the person believing in him with that of a new mother: "When a woman is in travail she has sorrow, because her hour has come; but when she is delivered of the child, she no longer remembers the anguish, for joy that a child is born into the world" (John 16:21).

We still remember pain. Don't others?

For each of us the experience of childbirth differs. Those for whom cesarean section is necessary have one kind of experience. Women having the opportunity to train themselves in natural childbirth methods have another.

For those able to relax during contractions, the process of giving birth is usually good. Others, for a variety of reasons, may have had a bad experience.

Sometimes problems in childbirth make us appreciate our baby even more. But we may also experience resentment, and if that is the case, we need to get our feelings out in the open.

Our first instincts may be against it. Take Julie, for instance. She had a difficult delivery. When her roommates began talking about their experiences, she turned away, the memory of pain clouding her eyes.

Later she said, "I resented that they had easier births. I didn't want to listen. I didn't want to talk about it. I only wanted to shout, 'I'll never have another baby.' "

It's only natural to try to submerge our fear and resentment if we've had a difficult experience. Yet the deeper the impression, the more we hurt ourselves by pushing down our feelings. The harder we work to keep our emotions inside, the more numb we seem to go on the surface.

Small wonder, if we are working to deny negative feelings, that we are unable to feel positive ones. Small wonder that not every mother is able to feel instant joy about her baby.

That's why it's important to find a person who understands—who will let us work out the feelings we're trying to keep inside. As one woman said, "I needed to verbalize my reactions, to get them into the open."

Often it helps just to have an honest conversation. But after we've talked everything through, God can give us deeper cleansing. He offers us the opportunity to pray, "Lord, forgive me for the resentment I feel about the persons or circumstances that have hurt me. Reach down into my mind and emotions and spirit. Take away my memory of pain, or change it into something productive."

In praying for inner healing, we ask God to bind our wounds, making ragged memories whole, so we can feel joy about our baby and begin to grow in our love.

Fortunately, God is a Person before whom we can be completely honest any time of the day or night. He does not say to us, "You should feel this way" or "You should feel that way." He does not push us or try to hurry us beyond our ability. We mothers find a promise in the 40th chapter of Isaiah. The Shepherd will "gently lead those that are with young."

To be gently led means to be taken at the pace best for us. If we are ready, it means feeling love for our infant at once. But if we are not, it means growing in love after our own needs are met.

To be gently led means to be brought into a pasture where we know the joy made possible for us by Christ because we have been honest about the path which brought us there. Some reach that pasture the moment after birth; for others, reaching is delayed.

To be gently led also means to feel our husband's arms around us, to feel free to ask to be held if he doesn't do it spontaneously or sense our need, to realize that being held is part of the healing process.

For most of all, to be gently led means to be brought into a sense of being loved with a love that seeks the best for us—with a love that infuses us with warmth, melting each cold spot in our heart, until we are able to reach out once again.

For then, as we take our newborn in our arms, we will clasp that infant to us with the depth of our own love.

Lead me, Shepherd, lead me
through whatever pastures
you know I need.

If I need healing,
bring me to a spring of your making
and cleanse my wounds.

If I need love,
bring me to a view of your mountains
and the knowledge that in your strength
there is also tenderness.

If I need joy,
bring me to your meadow of soft grass
and wild flowers blowing in the wind.

For in your healing, your love, and your joy
I will find beauty.
And each of these I will offer
to my child.

4

Little Miss Muffet

One morning when our youngest son was five, I entered his bedroom and found him struggling to pull on his stockings. "When I get bigger I'll get farther away from my feet," he said. "Then I'll have to keep my socks on all the time."

I smiled and explained that his arms would grow as his legs lengthened. Yet his words reminded me of an evening five years before, shortly after he had been born. I had been too busy feeling sorry for myself to have a sense of perspective.

It had been a day in which I had experienced the high of laughter, for the nurses had combed the long hair of my infant down over his forehead so it touched his eyebrows. Yet it had also been a day in which I had felt exhaustion. I had longed to nap, but hospital noises kept me awake.

As evening came, I noticed a spider spinning a web far up in the corner closest to my bed. While I watched the trap grow larger, my irritation increased. Unafraid of spiders, I normally had no problem getting rid of them. If I had only had a broom, Mrs. Spider would have disappeared with one whack. Instead, she remained out of reach, catching me in a web of frustration.

In my mind I summed up my annoyance. At last I have time to rest, I thought, and I have to look at a cobweb. And even worse, the nurses will bring my new little son into a room with a spider.

For a moment I remembered the bedroom I had prepared for him at home—its freshly painted blue walls, its recently laundered curtains, its snug bassinet with clean white sheets.

An inner part of me realized how ridiculous I was being, but I was too tired and weak to cope, and that night when the lights were out, my body shook with sobs. I tried to cry quietly, afraid that my roommate or a nurse would hear, afraid they would ask, "What's the matter?" Because I knew I would have to say, "There's a spider in the corner."

Like our famous Miss Muffet, I was seeing something small and reacting out of proportion to its importance. Like other women who experience blues shortly after childbirth, I was allowing something minor to become major. And even as I realized I was being silly, I couldn't help but cry.

Since then I have learned that while many new mothers remain emotionally calm, others go through highs and lows. Some tend to weep more easily than they normally would, often without a conscious reason. As one young woman said, "Seeing my husband hold the baby brought tears—but that wasn't unusual. Everything did for a couple of days."

In my case I felt better after one good cry. The following afternoon I was able to go home and get the sleep and supportive love I needed. But sometimes the process of getting things in perspective is gradual, tempered by physical strength or weakness.

We may feel frustrated or let down after the months of looking ahead to childbirth. "What an empty feeling!" (Sometimes good—we can tie our shoes again—but sometimes bad.)

The physiological changes our body is going through may bother us. Perhaps a visitor wasn't as excited about our newborn as we had hoped. Or we may feel unable to cope with the details required to care for a family.

Whatever the cause, we are struggling to pull on our socks, thinking that our arms are too short to reach.

In *The Joy of Natural Childbirth,* Helen Wessel mentions the importance of having prolactin, a woman's built-in "tranquilizer," released into the bloodstream by a breast-feeding baby. She writes:

> Many women have admitted a "baby-blues" period during the early weeks, when all the changes of daily life seem just too much. But there are honest, aware-of-themselves women who say, "Yes, a cloud of gloom did descend. But I just nursed my baby, and it went away!"

Some new mothers find the Psalms have special meaning. When David experienced the blues, he wrote, "Pity me, O Lord, for I am weak. Heal me, for my body is sick, and I am upset and disturbed. My mind is filled with apprehension and with gloom. Oh, restore me soon" (Ps. 6:2-3 LB).

In Psalm 40 he added, "I waited patiently for God to help me; then he listened and heard my cry. He lifted me out of the pit of despair, out from the bog and the mire, and set my feet on a hard, firm path and steadied me as I walked along. He has given me a new song to sing, of praises to our God" (Ps. 40:1-3 LB).

With most new mothers, tears become smiles when they are strong enough to leave home, and a thoughtful friend says, "Why don't you do something *you'd* like to do for a couple of hours? I'll take care of the baby." Or if a husband suggests, "Let's call a sitter and go out for dinner." Loving support is the foundation for feeling able to cope.

For people such as these, the tendency to weep usually fades gradually away. Only occasionally do postpartum blues develop into a depression lasting for several weeks. In that case two symptoms may develop: loss of interest in things a person normally likes to do (such as going to a concert or buying new clothes); and inability to get important things done (such as caring for a child). If these symptoms occur, it would be beneficial to talk with a doctor or a pastor.

Yet for most of us, the feeling of crying too easily disappears with time. As our emotions steady, we experience the joy of having a newborn child. We learn we can put on our socks without struggling. We no longer feel caught in a web, because we are strong enough to frighten the spider away!

Lord, sometimes contradicting emotions
swell the circumstances of my life
until they seem beyond my reach and control.
Be with me when the tears come.
Give me the loving support I need.
Create in me a sense of perspective
so that everyday events
come within arm's length once again.

5

Chosen mother chosen child

Our daughter Gail was nearly five when my husband Roy and I were married. Standing next to me at the altar, she clutched her basket of flowers, her wispy dark hair forming ringlets on her flushed cheeks. Peering around my lace skirt, she swayed forward on tiptoes, watching intently as Roy and I exchanged rings.

For weeks she had proudly told everyone, "Daddy and I are getting married to Loie." Now, in her pink and white flowergirl's dress, surrounded by candlelight and roses, she watched her wish become reality.

Since that time people have often asked me, "Are you Gail's stepmother?" Even yet something within me recoils at the word. No, I am not a stepmother in the misused, fairy-tale sense of the word. I like the term "second mother," or better yet, "chosen mother," for during our marriage ceremony I became the person God used as the result of countless prayers—prayers said even by Gail herself.

On a spring morning nearly two years after her mother's death, Gail came to my sister-in-law Helen, who had invited Roy to live in her home so she could care for Gail. We had not yet told Gail that Roy and I wanted to be married. She knew me only as a friend. But God spoke through the security Helen had provided, creating in Gail a sense of need for a new kind of relationship. That morning she asked Helen, "Won't you be my very own mommy?"

"I have to be a mommy for my children, too," Helen reminded gently. "But you *could* have your very own mommy."

Gail's brown eyes sparkled. "I'd like that," she answered.

"Well, let's talk to God about it, shall we?" Helen suggested.

Gail's small head bowed, her eyelids crinkled shut, as she earnestly asked for a mommy of her own.

That night she met Roy at the door. "It's all settled," she announced. "You can marry Loie!"

Through marriage some of us are chosen mothers. Through adoption others of us receive a chosen child. Each of us has special moments connected with the "how" of our status, but all of us who become mothers through marriage or adoption know the many pieces that must fit into the puzzle before it becomes a picture.

In our case God brought Roy from Albuquerque to Milwaukee and then to Minneapolis so we could meet. Others know another kind of introduction. As one adoptive father said, "It's a heavy feeling when you walk down a corridor and know that on the other side of that door you're meeting a responsibility that will be yours for at least 18 to 20 years."

Some adoptive parents know the nervous anticipation of an airport arrival. Friends of ours cherish a photo snapped by a reporter during the moment they received their Vietnamese baby. While the mother holds her baby for the first time, tears of joy stream down her cheeks. The father looks on, his hand reaching forward to cup the baby's head.

"If our son ever wonders if we wanted him, we'll just show him that picture," he said.

As our ways of meeting vary, so too does our preparation. For some the waiting time is fairly short, for others long, with a last-minute scramble at the end. Regardless of how we receive our child, our feelings about our qualifications for motherhood are important.

I was fortunate to have the opportunity of becoming acquainted with Gail gradually, learning her needs and her likes and dislikes. Even so, during those first months after marriage I'd often think, "I don't know what to do. If I were her biological mother, I'd *know*."

Adoptive mothers frequently express the same feeling about their new babies. "I feel clumsy—just plain nervous about being a mother," they sometimes say. "But for biological mothers it's instinctive, isn't it? Because of the time in the womb?"

It was only after I had two biological children that I could say with certainty, "No, mothering isn't instinctive because of the birth process. For some women it may be easier than for others. But it is not in *how* we achieve our status that motherhood comes. It is a quality within us that develops as we care for a child."

It would have helped me to know our daughter since infancy. Then I could have grown with her.

But for those of us who are adoptive parents, the seed of motherhood begins to grow as we experience a longing for a child of our own. As husband and wife become one physically to create a biological child, so adoptive couples become one emotionally in their desire to choose a child of their own.

Then our ability to mother develops as we share our time, our thoughts, and our energy. Even as biological mothers learn to diaper and feed their firstborn, we also discover how to provide for the needs of our child, whatever the age.

Whether we receive a child by birth or adoption, our ability to love is the same. In caring for a child we grow in that love, even as a biological parent does. Our love deepens, becoming greater as we give. One adoptive mother put it well: "My baby didn't grow under my heart but in it."

Out of that very love, we who are adoptive or chosen mothers may regret that we were not able to know our children for every moment of their lifetime (except, perhaps, during two A.M. feedings). Yet we don't need to dwell on that regret. Through deep appreciation of our children as unique individuals, we can make up for whatever moments we lost in the minutes that are now. As one new mother said, "I coffeed every day for a week, I was so eager to show my baby to everyone."

That same love can lay to rest any twinges we may have about the stepmother image created by Grimm's fairy tales. Being overly sensitive about reactions of people around us doesn't help our parenting. We need to believe that out of our love we are doing our very best.

"I was afraid to get after my four-year-old in front of other people," commented one adoptive mother. "And sometimes just a bit of firmness would have taken care of the situation. But instead I was wondering about what people would think of *me*."

Whether our children are chosen or biological, their need for consistent discipline is the same. Whichever way our children come to us, we will rejoice in their future successes and hurt with them in their failures. It's not the moment of birth that makes us mothers. What counts is our commitment to our children, our faith in the rightness of their being ours, and our love for them as individuals created by God.

In Luke 9:48 Christ stood a young child beside him and said, "Anyone who takes care of a little child like this is caring for me! And whoever cares for me is caring for God who sent me. Your care for others is the measure of your greatness" (LB).

As Paul writes in 1 Corinthians 13, "So faith, hope, love abide, these three; but the greatest of these is love." If we give our children, whether chosen or biological, this gift of love, we wrap our arms around them with the best we can offer.

I know, for I have been blessed both ways.

Thank you, Lord, for enriching our love
with our unity of thought.

Thank you for blessing the oneness
of our desire to parent a child.

In this moment when we become mother and father
give us your added blessing.
Let us feel the excitement,
yet also the responsibility.
Let us treasure this sunlit first time
when we hold the child you have given us,
and the joy welling up, spilling over,
tells us this gift is ours!

6

In the shelter
of his hand

A German deaconess, Sister Dorothea Steigerwald, has sculpted a clay statue of a hand reaching upward, palm open. A small girl leans into the center of the hand as the fingers curl slightly, cradling her head and body.

In the shelter of the hand she is content, at rest. But behind the statue stretches the shadow of a cross.

Appropriately named *Bleib Sein Kind* ("Remain His Child"), the statue speaks to those who are children at any age. Most of us have times in our lives when we long for a supporting hand. When we look at our newborn we may think, "Will I be able to handle that fragile bundle?" or "Will the umbilical cord open if I touch it wrong?"

Our feelings of inadequacy may increase as we realize how dependent a nursing infant is on us. We wonder, "Is my baby getting enough milk?"

Then, when we go home from the hospital, our newborn starts crying, much longer it seems than ever before.

That same crying will bother us if we're adoptive

parents. Although probably older, our new bundle still will waken feelings of uncertainty.

During the following weeks, there may be other times when the baby fusses for what seems forever. "It really makes me feel good if I can figure out what's wrong," said one mother. "But it gets me down if I can't."

Then someone else offers to hold our recent arrival, and instantly the baby stops crying. What did we do wrong?

Cultural pressures may add to the feelings of inadequacy we already sense. Every time we pick up a mother's magazine we are assailed by the importance of our influence during the early years. "In one year, you can easily raise your child's IQ by 10 to 16 points," says an ad in a new mother's magazine. Soon we find ourselves asking, "Am I being adequately creative? Am I providing a stimulating environment?"

It *is* important to pick up our child, giving our baby skin contact, talking and encouraging response. It *is* important to cuddle an infant during feedings. But don't we do those things naturally if our sense of inadequacy or our feeling of being pressed for time doesn't get in the way?

Sometimes we feel pushed because outside forces are imposing certain standards on us; other times we feel pushed because we are expecting too much of ourselves. That brings us to the question: What quality is the most important in our mothering? Perhaps we would unanimously answer, "Love!" If so, we need to give thought to whatever will encourage the spontaneous flow of that love.

We might ask ourselves, "Is my baby really as

fragile as I think?" Some infants, such as those born prematurely, require special handling. Yet we generally underestimate a baby's strength.

A day or two after our first son was born, I strolled down the hospital corridor to stand outside the nursery window. There I noticed how our son's tiny bed and his seven-pound body contrasted with the size of adults moving in the hallway.

"I don't know if I can handle him," I thought. "How about his bath? I'll drop him for sure."

But only a few hours later one of the nurses told me, "We're giving a demonstration tomorrow for all mothers who would like to come. Do you mind if we use your baby to show how to give a bath?"

I was delighted, and the next day found myself in the front row. Before me was a table on which all the bathing things had been neatly assembled. An efficient-looking nurse walked in, carrying my sleeping newborn, football-style under one arm.

When she unwrapped his blanket, he awoke. While she undressed him, he started to cry. As she washed his face and hair, he began to scream.

As his long, white-blond hair dried, it stood out around his head like the down of a baby chick. But there any semblance of softness ended, for his arms and legs flailed the air and his chest expanded as his small face and then his body turned purple with rage.

In that moment my feelings of inadequacy vanished. "Good!" I thought gleefully. "If he screams like that for a nurse bathing babies every day, then it's fine if he cries for me!"

But bathing times soon became special, not only for the baby as he learned to enjoy his bath, but also for me. Best of all was the moment when I held him to me, neatly wrapped again, and I smelled his clean hair and buried my nose in his soft little neck.

Often, through experience, feelings of inadequacy vanish like soapy water going down the drain. In their place we know confidence. That quality of confidence can mean the difference between success and failure if we desire to breast-feed our baby.

Looking to our own needs for balanced diet, intake of fluids, and proper rest and relaxation will encourage our production of milk. Frequent breast-feeding usually provides the stimulation needed to produce more. (It is more important to nurse frequently than to allow the baby to spend a long time at the breast.)

Yes! We can get the air bubble up so our baby is comfortable.

And, yes! It's okay if our infant stops crying when taken by someone else. They're not as tired or tense as we are.

Yet other times our feelings of inadequacy are not so easy to handle. What about those moments?

We never will feel totally in control of every situation we confront. But feelings of inadequacy can also be an asset, for they remind us of our need for someone stronger, for someone outside ourselves.

A long time ago God sent a baby into this world—a child just as fragile, yet just as strong as the one we brought home. Because that baby grew to adulthood, the shadow of a cross stretches behind the child leaning into the protective hand. Because of that cross we are able to claim the words of Paul:

Now God says he will accept and acquit us—declare us "not guilty"—if we trust Jesus Christ to take away our sins. And we all can be saved in this same way, by coming to Christ, no matter who we are or what we have been like. Yes, all have sinned; all fall short of God's glorious ideal; yet now God declares us "not guilty" of offending him if we trust in Jesus Christ, who in his kindness freely takes away our sins (Rom. 3:22-24 LB).

Many of us, as little children, trusted in Jesus Christ. Yet somewhere during the intervening years we drifted away from him. If that was the case, we can pray, "Lord, I know I am sinful. And I know that you have provided a way to help me. Will you forgive me? I trust in your power to save me."

In saying those words we receive God's resource for eternal life. Yet we also open the floodgates for the abundance he has promised to give us now.

If we find it hard to trust, we can ask for that ability, for that too is a gift from God. In consciously turning over our feelings of inadequacy, we depend on him for both our eternal and daily needs.

We are simply leaning into the shelter of his hand.

Thank you, Lord,
that you don't mind being bothered,
that you want me to rest
in the promise of your care.

If I am too sure of myself,
show me my need.
If I am too proud to trust,
break down my defenses.
If I am too afraid to believe,
show me your kindness,
but also your strength.

Lord, I ask your forgiveness;
I accept your love.
You are *with me!*
That is all I need.
You are *in me—*
my strength in every weakness.

Keep me trusting, ever leaning
into the shelter of your hand.

7

Wisdom of the heart

Each time I became a patient on the obstetric floor of a hospital, I looked forward to certain minutes in the daily routine. I learned to listen for the rubber heels of nurses padding down the hallway. When feeding time drew near, I anticipated the arrival of my baby and the opportunity to cuddle his warm body next to mine. I found joy in cradling his silken head in my arms and watching his first attempts to nurse.

All of us who are mothers, whether adoptive or biological, enjoy watching our children eat, seeing bony legs fill out and thin little hands become chubby. Yet even while we observe their development, we become aware of our personal need for growth of another kind. As one mother put it, "When I thought about my responsibility for my baby's growth, I realized there was something missing in my own life."

Peter must have noticed a similar lack in the lives of his scattered Christian friends. He wrote to them, "Long to grow up into the fullness of your salvation;

cry for this as a baby cries for his milk" (1 Peter 2:3 LB).

Every mother is well aware of how that first squall sounds, piercing the darkness of night. We know how demanding the cry of a baby can be. Yet is our longing for spiritual growth that desperate?

In his letter to the Corinthians, Paul tells them to develop their spiritual appetites. "I cannot talk to you as I would to healthy Christians, who are filled with the Spirit," he says. "I have had to feed you with milk and not with solid food, because you couldn't digest anything stronger" (1 Cor. 3:1-2 LB).

When we add solid food to a child's diet, we realize that their ability to digest cereal or applesauce means they have reached a new stage of development. In the same way, the digestion of solid spiritual food adds a dimension to our motherhood.

But our first question may be, "How can I squeeze out any spare moments for my own growth?" Often we feel overwhelmed by endless feedings and constant interruptions. Yet perhaps when we are the most rushed we can best appreciate the value of flash prayers.

We can start out the day by giving ourselves and our loved ones to God. It may have to be a quick, "I give the day to you, Lord," as we jump out of bed, trying to reach our infant before cries wake everyone else. Even so, we can reaffirm that commitment at odd moments during the day.

Our diapering minutes can be a reminder to say, "God, bless my baby. Thank you for giving my child the ability to function normally." Frequent feedings can be the opportunity to pray, "Lord, be with my growing child. Help me give the needed guidance."

In our search for a good meal, we turn to the source through which spiritual food flows. Many new mothers like to read while they are nursing or holding a bottle. "When my children were infants, I found that my best moments to receive spiritual nourishment came while they were taking in physical nourishment," said one.

Even if we have time for only one verse, we can store its meaning in our hearts, thinking about it, as Mary treasured the events surrounding the arrival of the shepherds.

Middle-of-the-night feedings may offer the only quiet time we have for awhile. Yet even in our half-awakeness we can call on the promise given in the first chapter of James. If we don't know what to do, we can simply ask God, and he will give us a bountiful supply of wisdom. "But," we are told, "when you ask him, be sure that you really expect him to tell you, for a doubtful mind will be as unsettled as a wave of the sea that is driven and tossed by the wind" (James 1:6 LB).

As Solomon requested wisdom for serving his people, we can seek an understanding mind to better help our families. Moreover, we can ask for a wisdom mixed with one cup of common sense and many cups of love.

During the kindergarten year of our second child, his teacher wanted him to tell her the date of his birth, the place, and the time. Our son asked me to write down the details, but the next morning after he left for school I realized I had forgotten. When he returned that afternoon, I met him at the door and asked what he had done about giving his teacher the information.

"Oh, it was okay, Mom," he answered. "I hearted it."

If something is important to us, we are able to find room for it in our hearts. As our children grow physically, we can mature spiritually, treasuring each learning moment we are given. When we trust God to provide the wisdom we need, as we need it, we are able to hold before us a vision of the young life we cradle in our arms. We can anticipate the tomorrow when that child will depend on us for more than physical food.

Those of us who seek to feed others can also be fed ourselves, not just for one meal, nor even for a hundred, but for a lifetime.

Thank you, Lord,
for preparing a banquet table
to satisfy the needs of my inner self.
Thank you for offering your loaves
of love and wisdom and knowledge.
Develop in me a hunger to grow,
a longing for an understanding mind,
so that in the years ahead
I will sense my need
to eat daily of your spiritual bread.

8

With a breath
of kindness

One of the memory-building moments surrounding
the gift in our arms comes when it's time to take our
baby home.

As we prepare to leave the hospital, we bend over
the bed, dressing our newborn—bringing wiggly arms
through tiny sleeves, fumbling with snaps or zippers or
incredibly small buttons, tying the ribbons of a recently
received cap, folding the blanket just so across a little
chest—aware all the time of the importance of this first
visit to the outside world.

For those who are adoptive mothers, that moment
arrives when we stretch out our arms to accept the
anticipated bundle. The dreamlike quality of our decision vanishes before reality. The miracle of having our
own baby begins. We clasp our child to our breast,
releasing the pent-up emotions of months of waiting.

Yet, however exciting the time of receiving has been,
our down-to-earth life with the child in our arms begins
when our car pulls up to the back door. As on our
marriage night, we cross a threshold. On the other side

we begin to build friendships in the hearts of each member of our newly enlarged family.

We soon realize that every child who enters our home offers endless possibilities for enriching our lives. At the moment, however, we may not feel very rich. We may be weak or tired. We may be nervous or tense. And the one demanding the most attention is no doubt our new baby. At least that's the person making the most noise.

If we are tired or tense, our recent arrival will no doubt sense that, as well as the change in surroundings. If our baby shows a grasp of the situation through hearty noises, that's fine. Our infant is simply showing intelligence. (And if our child doesn't cry, that shows intelligence too.)

Yet, if we already have other sons or daughters, they are the most important right now. We can hardly wait to cuddle them, to put the baby on a small lap, to let our older children carefully hold the blanket-wrapped bundle.

In the days that follow our homecoming, we renew our relationships with our older children. As one mother said, "I worried about my feelings toward my daughter, wondering if they would change because she was no longer my baby. And yes, my feelings *did* change. They deepened and strengthened."

As mothers, we learn very quickly that what we really want is the glow of friendship within our home —friendship that fosters openness and trust between every member of the family, yet retains the status of motherhood so we can correct and guide our children.

An Arabian proverb tells us:

A friend is one
to whom one may pour
out all the contents of one's heart,
chaff and grain together,
knowing that the gentlest of hands
will take and sift it,
keep what is worth keeping
and with a breath of kindness
blow the rest away.

As mothers who are also friends, we offer gentle hands, appreciating the individuality of each child and each stage of growth. "I'm not in a hurry for my second baby to do this or that as I was with my first," explained one mother. "I just enjoy him one day at a time."

Those same gentle hands offer love to whatever older children we have. We appreciate the protectiveness of other sons or daughters toward the baby. We show them how the baby can grab a finger, curling its own small fingers around it.

When our new arrival sits in an infant seat, we tell our older children, "Do you see how the baby watches you longer than the rest of us? She looks as though she can hardly wait to be big enough to play with you."

As mothers who are friends, we offer, too, our listening ability. We listen for the outward needs of our older children. But we listen also for inward hurts, hidden cries.

So much has been said about sibling jealousy that sometimes it is overemphasized. If we give children the feeling that we expect them to be jealous, they no doubt will be. If we give them security and love, along with appreciation of their uniqueness, they won't need to be.

Sometimes a jealous child is simply reacting the way we would if we felt left out. Other times that child needs guidance in realizing that much of life involves learning to share.

When we find it difficult to achieve the hairline balance, it helps to pray, "Lord, show me where to concentrate. Show me what to notice. Make me aware of the needs of all my children. Then give me your creativity in helping to meet those needs."

As mothers who are also friends, we attempt to build a network of love—not only between ourselves and our children, but also between the children themselves. Each of us will find individual ways to encourage this.

Our daughter was seven when our first son was born. In our efforts to make her feel good about the new arrival, my husband and I bought a doll she had wanted for some time. That doll became her gift "from the baby."

Two years later, when I became pregnant again, we made plans to build on our initial success. I decided to sew clothes in addition to the ones already belonging to the treasured doll. Before my due date, I made little dresses, skirts, blouses, and slacks. When I started labor, I took them out of hiding and slipped them into my suitcase.

Each time my husband visited me after the birth of our second son, he took one little item of clothing back to our daughter. Attached to each small gift was a note with a message such as, "To my new sister. I love you. Your baby brother, Kevin."

If those first moments are to be effective, they must be integrated into our lives in such a way that the pattern continues. I am grateful to visitors who realized that my baby wouldn't remember their oohs and ahs, but my older child would. They found out what she was doing and asked her to show them her room or her drawings.

Usually friends take the hint if a mother suggests that Susie or Johnnie has something to show. Grandparents can also help by holding older children and by taking time to read to them, particularly during the moments when we nurse or give the baby a bottle.

Sometimes balanced thoughtfulness averts regression in an older child when a baby enters the family—but not always. One mother complained, "Whatever my son knew, he doesn't know now."

If an older child regresses, we don't need to feel that the problem will last forever. When aware that we appreciate bigness as much as smallness, our son or daughter will take on responsibilities again. That's a promise! (Have you ever seen a 15-year-old of normal capabilities still being dressed by mother?)

As mothers who are also friends, part of our job includes sifting the chaff and the grain, recognizing good and poor behavior, knowing when to encourage and when to correct. Through our encouragement we can keep what is worth keeping, and with the firmness that is a breath of kindness, we can blow the rest away.

An older mother once told a friend of mine, "You're not used to being a parent yet." My friend was grateful for the comment, for she realized she needed a better understanding of what type of behavior to expect at each stage of a child's development. She became less irritated with the typicalness of her children's reactions. While learning which things are important to notice, she began to trust in God's ability to help her mother.

In spite of our best efforts, our children aren't always going to behave the way they should. They won't always love each other as we would like.

Yet we can prepare our homes to be places in which God acts. When the pressure of trying to develop friendships becomes too much, we can pause for one moment, saying, "God, I love you," or "God, I praise you for what you mean in my life."

We don't have to be in a good mood to utter those prayers. We don't need an emotional high. We can simply pray the words with our minds, repeating them until God works the miracle, bringing our emotions into line.

For coming home is, after all, simply a matter of sensing God's presence within us. Those of us who seek to be friends as well as mothers often feel the need for that greater friendship.

A long time ago the children of Israel complained that the Lord had forgotten them and his promise of a covenantal relationship. Speaking through the prophet Isaiah, God asked: "Can a woman forget her sucking child, that she should have no compassion on the son of her womb?" Even during moments when our children behave their worst, we find that idea hard to accept.

But yes, admits the next verse, some women *can* forget their children. And with that acknowledgment God promises, "Even these may forget, yet I will never forget you" (Isa. 49:15).

When we are groping for friendships in our home, we can relax in our parenting, resting in the promise that we too are being held in the gentlest of hands, that God will "keep what is worth keeping and with a breath of kindness blow the rest away."

Thank you, Lord,
for being willing to come into my home,
for promising that you will never forget me.

Through your friendship
inspire in me an awareness of the inner and outer needs
of each member of my family.
Help me to be a mother who is also a friend,
a listener who gives love and yet firmness
when each of those is needed.

Teach me, Lord,
how to blow the chaff but keep the grain
in the lives of those around me.

9

Out of his
treasure house

In addition to the new baby and older children, if they
are present, there are yet other strands to be woven
into the fabric of our enlarging family. When a baby
comes into our home, we realize in a new way the truth
of the words, "When you marry someone, you marry
the entire family."

Our extended family includes parents, sisters, broth-
ers, aunts, uncles, and all the in-laws. We learn very
quickly that these relationships change when children
are present. We hope that means the bonds will be
strengthened, so our relatives will be among our closest
friends.

As mothers, we know that each of our relationships
offers the opportunity for variety in the pattern we are
weaving. But during the months surrounding the arrival of a child, we find that parents play an especially
important part in our lives. It meant a great deal to me
that after the birth of each of our sons, my mother-in-
law came to help. Those were weeks when she did

everything she could to let me know that she loved and supported me.

If we are fortunate enough to enjoy that kind of relationship, we know that one of the greatest gifts another person can offer is to believe in us. As Charles Morgan has said, "There is no surprise more wonderful than the surprise of being loved; it is God's finger on man's shoulder."

Throughout the years my mother-in-law has continued in the pattern she began in those early days. On one occasion when my husband and I needed encouragement she wrote, "I fully believe in you. We'll just keep enjoying each other and pull together." Yet during those early years I often wondered if I asked too much by having her come to help me.

All of us are aware of the problems involved if we don't respect the right of our parents to be independent. But since that time I've come to realize how much I want to be included when the day comes for my own grandchildren to be born.

Usually when a biological child enters our home, we ask for that kind of help, simply because we need it. However, when we adopt a baby the situation is a bit different. After the new one arrives, we don't need to regain strength lost through childbirth. Often, because there is no physical need for help, we forget to include our parents.

"I didn't think of this until I sat in on a conversation between several older women," said a mother of four. "One grandmother remarked, 'I'm going to help my daughter as soon as her next one comes.' Another answered, 'So am I. Her baby's due in April.' But the woman who had just received an adoptive grandchild didn't say a word. Her look told me that she felt left out."

If we are adoptive parents, we may find that another generation has a different attitude toward adoption than we have. Yet we stand in the middle between a new generation and an older one, laying stepping stones.

Often the stream can be crossed by the children themselves. When one baby smiled at her new grandfather, he remarked, "I think the baby's going to like me." He felt included.

Whatever strands we are weaving, we can remember the rich bass voice of Richard Evans as he said, "You who have any to love you, cling to them and thank God."

This is a time of pattern-making, a time when we want to weave in rich traditions our parents gave us, a time when we want to encourage the ongoing quality of the generations.

Couples living long distances from parental homes often sense the need for grandparents so much that they seek out substitutes.

Those of us with accessible parents find that another generation offers a heritage of wisdom and knowledge which we ourselves are not yet prepared to give. Our children love the moments when a grandparent sits down and says, "Do you want to hear about a time when your daddy was little? Or about when your mommy was *young?*"

But in order to have the sharing days that surround a new arrival or the supportive years that follow, we need to accept not only the love, but also the limitations involved in any relationship. No matter how carefully we push the shuttle back and forth, we discover places where the strands don't fall into the pattern we would like. We realize, too, that in some situations we can not go to a person who has hurt us and talk it out. We would only make matters worse.

Yet there is something we *can* do.

Many have written about the one-sided prayer of forgiveness. I like to call it the "Father, forgive them" prayer because it involves a sentence uttered by Christ as he hung on the cross. He spoke those words, not about polite, well-meaning people, as our friends and relatives usually are, but about people who were mocking even his death as they divided his clothing.

In countless ways I have tested that petition and found it valuable in everyday life. Sometimes I have prayed, "Father, forgive them" when I scarcely meant the words. Yet I simply said, "Lord, I ask you to forgive the person who hurt me. In the name of Jesus, I ask you to bless that person."

Often I have felt as though I were following only empty form. Certainly my emotions weren't behind the words. But here again, as in seeking the presence of God, it's a matter of praying with the will. Then God steps in and changes our emotions, removes our resentments, and fills us with peace and love.

In this regard Christ reminds us: "If you forgive the sins of any, they are forgiven; if you retain the sins of any, they are retained" (John 20:23).

In the Living Bible his words read: "If you forgive anyone's sins, they are forgiven. If you refuse to forgive them, they are unforgiven."

If we forgive, we offer God the opportunity to begin working in the life of any person who has injured us.

49

We also allow God to replace our bitterness or resentment with something better.

Praying the "Father, forgive them" prayer is seldom easy. Living in the attitude of forgiveness is to experience Christ's cruicifixion daily—to offer our egos, our pride, our selfishness, our defensiveness, even as he offered his life.

To live in the attitude of forgiveness is also to live in the attitude of acceptance—not acceptance of wrong, but acceptance of the fact that God is the one to make changes in another individual if they are needed.

A wise person once said, "We try to be gods instead of God's." To be God's means to believe in his pattern-changing ability. In her paraphrase of 1 Corinthians 13:5-7, Grace Magney has written:

> Really liking people is accepting everyone for what he is, believing the best in doubtful situations, hoping for God's pattern to unfold in the other's life and waiting as long as God before you give him up.

Because of the cross we can accept. Because of the cross we can forgive. Because of the cross we can be used in weaving beautiful patterns in areas of our lives needing more love.

In Philippians 4:19 Paul writes, "And my God will supply every need of yours according to his riches in glory in Christ Jesus."

God doesn't manage a fabric department that runs out. From his treasure house he offers strands of red or purple, blue or green, brown, gold, or silver.

We have only to ask.

Lord, even as you have accepted me,
forgiving my sins,
help me to accept others,
forgiving whatever hurts they have caused.

Thank you for not being content
with weaving only one strand or two,
but for wanting all my relationships
worked into a beautiful pattern.

Remind me to turn things over to you,
allowing your abundance to become
a vital fiber in the fabric of my life.

10

Mr. Sandman,
give me your dreams

I had cleaned his room that day, changed the sheets, and even washed the windows. But my satisfaction in the sparkle was short-lived.

In walked our six-year-old. Plopping down on the bed, where I had turned back the blankets for the night, he pulled off his hole-in-the-toe tennis shoe.

"Wow!" he exclaimed. "Look at all the sand I can carry in my sock."

Before I could stop him, he dumped it out, first on the clean sheets and then onto the floor.

As children, most of us learned that Mr. Sandman is a nice gentleman who brings happy dreams. But as mothers, we may feel he attacks us—especially on the days when we carry not only gritty particles under our eyelids but also bags of sand on our backs.

What about those times when we've been up most of the night? When the dishes are stacked high in the sink and the to-be-washed diapers even higher? When we feel that we can't get anything done, and that we'll never be organized again? In other words, what do we do when we are exhausted, crabby, and fed up?

First, it may be small comfort, but I don't know of a mother who has escaped having that kind of day.

Then, too, we need to remind ourselves that a vicious cycle can develop. When we are physically tired, it's more difficult to keep up with our work or to be organized. And when things are piling up all around us, it's hard *not* to be crabby or discouraged. Soon we feel as if we're running uphill inside a spinning wheel.

Perhaps the following suggestions by a variety of mothers will offer something that works for you.

"I try to anticipate," said Beth. "I'm starting to see things before they happen. At first we hit all the crises at once."

Because she had two babies close in age, she found that often they needed something simultaneously. "I'd have to choose quickly, deciding which child had the most important need," she continued. "But now I'm learning to meet needs before they get there."

In areas of safety for our babies or toddlers we realize how essential it is to see the possibility of danger and supply the well-known ounce of prevention. In other matters it is simply common sense to try to take as many wrinkles out of the day as possible.

For instance, Sara's baby always woke up starved after his morning nap. "I quickly learned to drop whatever I was doing to feed him immediately," she said. "If I did, I had a serene afternoon. If I didn't, he cried, swallowed air, and became full of gas. Then whatever food I gave him made him miserable the rest of the day." Other mothers find it important to burp the baby *before* feedings to be sure that milk does not rest on top of an air bubble.

While some feel a schedule restricts the freedom they once had, many new mothers decide that sticking to one enables them to get more done. Though desiring to do things quickly and efficiently, we usually find that interruptions by small children make it impossible.

It may help to set long- and short-range goals. Sometimes our sense of order must be something *in process,* an objective toward which we work.

We might like to follow as much of a schedule as we find comfortable, flexing it to suit our individual personalities. If we keep a goal before us, we are much more likely to get things done than if we simply hope we'll be organized.

When we try to reach goals, establishing a schedule that works for us, we'll probably find that our baby is remarkably adaptive. Often this can be seen when adoptive parents try to imitate the way things were done in the foster home.

One adoptive mother, Carole, tells of her experience. "It was impossible for us to follow the schedule the foster parents had. Our new arrival was tearing our home apart because her meals, her naps, and her bedtime fell during hours that just didn't work in our family.

"Then one of my friends said to me, 'You figure out *your* schedule and let your daughter work into it.' Within just two days, we were able to switch the baby's bedtime from ten-thirty to seven o'clock."

Many babies are this adaptable. Sandy felt her second child wasn't. "For awhile it was much easier just to stay home than to take weekend trips because my son became upset by change. Gradually he outgrew it.

"But that's where goal-setting comes in," she said. "I had in mind a goal I thought would work in our family. I also noticed our son had a certain rhythm of waking and sleeping, eating and eliminating, crying and being contented. At first I went along with him. Then gradually I worked his schedule and mine together."

Many mothers believe that what makes the difference between success and failure in dealing with an infant is the assurance a child senses in us. If we are unsure how to act, babies know it. If we are confident, they feel that also.

When we're too tired, however, we often lose whatever assurance we have. Then priorities become important. If possible, a nap should be at the top of the list. In Psalm 139:3 David expressed this need: "You chart the path ahead of me, and tell me where to stop and rest" (LB). It's easy to feel as if we must keep up all the activities we once pursued before the baby arrived. Yet time for enough rest is vital.

Mothers who are breast-feeding find a direct correlation between tension, lack of rest, and supply of milk. Most of us find it helps if we're able to lie down for even 15 minutes. We can tell ourselves, "It doesn't matter if the living room furniture is dusted. I'll do it tomorrow. It doesn't matter if someone wants me to serve on a committee. I'll do it when my baby is older."

Then we can breathe deeply, consciously relax, and, to borrow Helen Wessel's phrase, "meditate on making milk." (Her entire chapter on breast-feeding in *The Joy of Natural Childbirth* is excellent.)

Many adoptive mothers also find the need for more rest is sometimes overwhelming. One mentioned how she and her husband worked out a solution: "I know this isn't possible for every couple, but my husband and I trade sleep times on weekends. I get up at six on Saturday and keep the kids quiet while he sleeps until nine. On Sunday morning he does the same for me."

Another mother offered an additional hint: "I try to accept the things I cannot change."

What are some of those things?

"I know that in spite of my best efforts there will be days when things don't fall into place—when I can't get my children to nap at the same time, when I can't get enough sleep. For instance, when I've just brought a baby home from the hospital, or when he's teething or sick. It used to frustrate me, and I wasted energy on the way I felt. Sometimes I still feel that frustration, but it helps to realize that loss of sleep is simply a part of this time in my life."

As we recognize these years as a time when bed never felt so good, we may be tempted to look back to the carefree moments we once had. We remember how it felt to run on a beach, the sunlight warm on our skin, the sand spraying out beneath our feet.

Yet we don't have to look over our shoulder. If our relationship is right, we have access to a very practical energy. Paul describes it when he says, "This is my work, and I can do it only because Christ's mighty energy is at work within me" (Col. 1:29 LB).

I've propped up similar words on my blender, where I see them whenever I wash dishes: "The kingdom of God is not just talking; it is living by God's power" (1 Cor. 4:20 LB).

Living by his power means realizing that we don't have to wait for crises before relying on God. We can sense the indwelling presence of Christ every day.

Living by that power also means recognizing that God *wants* us to depend on the resources he provides. "I am the Lord, the God of all flesh," he says. "Is anything too hard for me?" (Jer. 32:27). Amazing as it seems, something which looks difficult really isn't if we allow him to deal with a situation.

On the shores of Lake Superior, there's a stretch of beach covered by two- and three-inch rocks washed flat and smooth by the waves. When my husband and I stopped there, we longed for soft sand on which to rest while we watched our children swim.

But as we lay down, the stones shifted around us, making hollows for our bodies. Already warmed by the sun, the rocks soon warmed us. What looked hard had become something pleasant.

Another Power had been at work.

I'm tired today, Lord—
so tired, in fact,
that I find it hard to concentrate
on what to say to you.
But thanks for understanding,
for knowing that I need your everyday power.

When I'm tempted to think
I can make it on my own,
help me realize that you want me
to live in your strength,
filled with your joy.

I turn everything over to you, Lord.
Thanks for making even the hard things easy.

11

Gift of the tide

The sun's red ball glimmered across the Pacific Ocean, then slipped below the waves lapping the coastline. Seated on one of the logs scattered along the beach, a young woman rocked back and forth, humming quietly as she lulled the infant in her arms to sleep.

While she watched, the incoming tide broke higher and higher. She stretched out her legs, her bare toes kneading the sand, waiting for the cool water to swirl over them. Yet, though the waves washed closer with each trip, they never reached far enough to touch her. Finally she stood up, still clasping her baby against her breast, and waded into the water.

Now and then we feel as if we are watching waves lapping against a coastline—waves that are never going to reach us. We have already discovered that each new child who enters the home brings a time of adjustment. (Not as much candlelight, for instance!) Whether the baby is the first, second, or third, we find that the roles of family members shift just a bit until each person settles into a groove once again.

Often during that shifting of roles we desperately need communication—with parents, with other children if we have them, and most of all with our husband.

We may learn that his family followed one pattern in rearing children and our family followed another. We may also discover that while children can bring us together, they can also cause strain on a marital relationship.

Occasionally our preoccupation and busyness with the baby becomes a wedge between us. And while some husbands complain that they feel shut out by the new arrival, there are wives who have similar feelings.

"My husband pays so much attention to the baby, that every once in awhile I wonder if he loves the baby more than me," said one new mother. "I know it's irrational to feel that way. But just the same, I do."

We may also be hesitant to share about what we're doing. As one housebound mother said, "Some days I feel as though I haven't had the input needed for good conversation."

Another commented, "When I'm with small children all day I look forward to talking with my husband when he gets home. But he's been talking business for eight hours and just wants quiet."

As we live together week after week, we sense the incoming tide. The waves of our conversation come close to a depth of meaning. Yet our words may have the wrong edge to them rather than the directness they need. Unfortunately, they do not touch where it matters, revealing our real feelings.

It's easy to stop talking about little things, and when we do, we stop talking about big things. We waste time and energy thinking, "If only this were different—"

The longer we follow that pattern, the harder it is to change. We need to leave the log we're sitting on and wade into the water. We need to say, "Hey, look—can we talk this over?"

Relationships develop only if we are willing to work at them. No relationship is perfect, but without communication there can be no relationship. More often than we'd like, that communication involves saying four difficult words: "Will you forgive me?"

Yet differences between us can help us grow together, becoming the impetus for strength rather than weakness. That strength develops as each of us trusts the other person's ability to listen and respond, as we demonstrate mutual regard for our fragile inner selves.

But in addition to our desire for conversation that cuts through a "Pass the celery, dear," we need *time* to talk. Many things interfere: activities, working hours, baby's demands. Children seem to have an inbuilt sense of poor timing. Every couple recalls instances when the baby woke up crying, destroying an intimate moment.

Most of us, at one time or another, express the wish of the mother who said, "I *need* more private time with my husband." It's important that we meet that need.

While at Gustavus Adolphus College, I took a marriage and family class from Dr. Floyd Martinson. One day he drew two circles on the board.

"As a couple becomes husband and wife this circle becomes one," he said. "And as children arrive, one circle after another enters the sphere of the large one.

"But sometimes the couple forgets that if they are

60

granted a long life together there eventually will come a time when the children leave home and only the circle containing the two of them remains. Too often during the years in between couples neglect this fact. They forget to enjoy one another as persons. And when they are alone once again, they look at each other and find they are strangers."

Yet it is possible to not only remain acquainted but to continually draw closer to one another.

"We put a high priority on babysitting in our budget," said one mother. "It feels good to be on a date—just the two of us, doing something together, not having the whole marriage focus on babies."

A second couple found it easier to get babysitters on Saturday morning than on Saturday night, and they began going out for breakfast together.

A couple with one infant and one toddler bought two back carriers. Each toting a child, they set off on long walks. Usually the combination of fresh air and movement lulled the children to sleep. Those were ideal moments for husband and wife to talk in depth.

A woman who has six children, all past the infant stage, discovered that her husband's weakness was hors d'oeuvres. Each Friday afternoon she prepared a special tray which the two of them enjoyed when he returned home.

Another wife (whose baby sleeps later than five A.M.) tells how she and her husband spend their first minutes awake. "As he holds me in his arms, we pray together. Those are special moments when we begin our day, not only by being together, but also by being with God."

This couple found that their intellectual, physical,

and emotional unity was enriched by a spiritual oneness. As marriage and prayer partners, they claimed the promise of Christ: "I also tell you this—if two of you agree down here on earth concerning anything you ask for, my Father in heaven will do it for you. For where two or three gather together because they are mine, I will be right there among them" (Matt. 18:19-20 LB).

Such agreement implies joining our spirits in common purpose. When we agree in prayer, we offer not only faith in God, but also commitment to each other. If we are honest before God, we speak of our most deeply felt needs, and we are forced to reveal something of ourselves. As a result, we reach a deeper level of openness in our human relationship.

By telling God our needs, we give him the opportunity to work in our lives. As his power changes us or changes our circumstances, we experience the help of which one mother spoke: "Our baby was always fretful right when my husband came home from work. We became more and more frustrated because that was a time we wanted to talk. When we prayed about it together, the problem dissolved—the baby stopped crying at that time of day."

Creating moments for each other may take effort and prayer, but it's worth it. In those moments we strengthen intellectually and spiritually the partnership we entered through marriage.

Though we can't reproduce the moonlight and roses stage of our courtship, we can achieve an even richer bond. As we work with our husband to find time for each other, our God-created love enriches our longing for the one human being who means the most to us.

For a time after childbirth we must wait for physical oneness. But as we come together in love once again, the art of communication moves beyond the realm of words into a sunburst of joy.

We are running headlong into the waves.

Lord, I want that sense
of water lapping over my feet—
the rush of joy that comes
when I meet something real.
For I want something real
and honest and growing
as I build a life with my husband.

Give me courage for the times
when our relationship needs to be worked at.
Give me grace for the times
when I need to ask forgiveness.
Give me love for the times
when I need to understand.
Give me—give him—give us
the awareness of your presence
in our home.

12

Do you love me?

In the Broadway musical *Fiddler on the Roof,* Tevye confronts his wife with the plaintive question, "Do you love me?" Again and again he asks, and Golde replies, half-teasing, half-scolding, reminding him of the countless things she has done for him. Finally she admits that after all the time they've lived together, she supposes she loves him.

Tevye responds, "It doesn't change a thing, but even so, after 25 years, it's nice to know."

One evening when our love was new, I turned to the man I would someday marry and asked the same question, "Do you love me?"

Quietly he answered, "Loie, don't ask me if I love you, for then you are concentrating on yourself and what you are receiving. Instead, say, 'I love you,' and, in turn, I will tell you how much you mean to me."

We may be noticing that our marital relationship is changing. During our courtship and first months of marriage, we spent a great deal of time becoming intimately acquainted. Then, as we began to plan for a child, the focus of our marriage shifted slightly.

As man and woman, we begin a relationship by

looking at each other. As husband and wife, we don't want to lose that loving awareness. Yet if our relationship is to be maintained, we need, in addition, to grow so that we look at something together.

In time we will no doubt feel the need of a shared interest outside our home. But during this moment, the something we look at together is the gift in our arms. As we watch our infants become toddlers and our toddlers become preschoolers, we delight in their physical growth. Yet we hope they also will experience emotional growth, a balanced love which seeks the best interest of others.

Through the closest possible human relationship, that of husband and wife, we have the opportunity to learn that quality. When motivation for loving is no longer self-centered, but concentrates on the well-being of the beloved, the woman leaves the girl behind.

If we learn this lesson well, our children will perceive the way we live, perhaps consciously, perhaps unconsciously. Whichever way it comes, we hope that for them, seeing becomes believing in a way of life.

In the 12th chapter of Luke, Christ offers a criterion for giving: "Every one to whom much is given, of him will much be required" (v. 48). Certainly we can count ourselves among those to whom much has been given. It follows, then, that from us much is required.

We're all tempted to give where it's most noticeable. Although we receive more honor and recognition for that kind of giving, it wasn't what Christ had in mind. What matters is that we give, not where it shows, but where it counts the most—in the privacy of our own home.

When our children are young, we often feel we

have to give too much. But that's the time the husband and wife who realize their need for mutual support have an advantage. As one couple expressed it through a quote on their wedding program: "May our love be like an arch, two weaknesses leaning together to form one strength."

In addition to the strength shared in the marital relationship, God provides an even greater resource. By offering us the love of his Spirit, he supplies an artesian well from which to drink. And that water is available just for the asking.

Learning to express affection is not easy for some. One father, who grew up in a family unaccustomed to speaking about love, knew he had a lack in his own life.

"Now and then we talked about it," said his wife. "Although he was naturally reticent, he wanted the relationships in our family to be different. Soon after we brought our first child home from the hospital, he began a nightly ritual. He stood beside the bassinet and spoke to the baby, saying, 'I love you. I love you.'

"I'm sure that at first he felt utterly ridiculous," she continued. "But by the time our son was old enough to understand what he was saying, my husband felt comfortable about expressing his love audibly."

Another mother mentioned a feeling similar to that described by pediatric nurses. "We noticed a definite difference among our three children in whether they liked being cuddled. We wanted all of them to be able to respond to love, so we spent extra time cuddling the one who didn't take naturally to it. Now she's just as responsive as the others."

Our Lord mentioned another side of giving: "If you

give, you will get! Your gift will return to you in full and overflowing measure, pressed down, shaken together to make room for more, and running over. Whatever measure you use to give—large or small—will be used to measure what is given back to you" (Luke 6:38 LB).

Countless people seek only to receive. Yet for the Christian, it is possible to swing too far the other way. We can become so used to sharing our time, our energy, and our resources with others that we don't develop our ability to receive. If a relationship is to grow, there must be receiving as well as giving on both sides. If we seek the growth of those to whom we give, we will allow them to help us when the occasion for turnabout arises.

In a husband-wife relationship we hope that this develops naturally, out of love. But in the adult-child relationship, chances are it *won't* occur spontaneously. More than likely, we will need to teach children to give as they have received.

In dealing with our children, we may also need to draw upon God's wisdom to find a balance between giving and being trampled upon. Finding that balance may be like walking a tightrope. Yet when we reach the other side, we will know our applause as warmth in the heart.

When we, as husband and wife, help our children love and give, our own relationship deepens. We have found the secret of growing to look at something together.

One evening when our oldest son was in fourth grade he stood at an upstairs window, watching the sun drop westward. As he turned away from the curtain, he looked up at me and asked, "Why are we here, Mom? We're on earth such a short time and then it's all over."

Yes, why are we here? To make the quality of our lives something that counts as a gift for others? Perhaps, also, to reach the point where we seek that quality? For then we will be willing to pray, "Lord, produce in me the love I need in order to give."

After Peter's denial and Christ's subsequent death and resurrection, Jesus asked him, "Do you love me?"

Peter answered, "Yes, Lord, you know that I love you."

Christ asked a second time and then a third, "Do you love me?"

Peter was grieved as he replied, "Lord, you know everything; you know that I love you."

And to him the Lord said, "Feed my sheep."

To the Christ who asks us the same question, we can only answer, "Yes, Lord."

For to love is to give.

Thank you, Lord, for not making love
something that is poured into a bottle
and stored away on a shelf
for the winter of a possible need.
Instead, your love frees mine,
giving me the ability
to receive
as well as to give.

Fill me, Lord.
Refill me daily
with a love that continues to grow
for all who gather
in the kitchen of my life.

13

Safe in deep water

Only two months before, we had moved into a new neighborhood. I could hardly wait to tell my news to the women gathered for coffee. "I'm pregnant — the baby's due in February," I said.

"You'll have to hook up to city water," answered one of my neighbors.

I stared at her. That wasn't quite the reaction I had expected to what I considered an announcement of joy. "What do you mean?" I asked.

"Just that," she repeated. "There hasn't been a baby born on this block without the parents having to hook up to city water."

"That's ridiculous," I told her. "There's not a thing wrong with our well."

But on a Saturday afternoon exactly three weeks after our third child was born, my husband sat in the living room, listening.

"That pump's been running a long time," he said. "I better check on it."

We soon discovered our neighbor was right. All the

diaper washing had proved too great a demand on our 18-year-old pump.

As much as we hated to spend the money right then, we knew we had no choice. We needed water. Soon we joined the other new parents who had debated, "Shall we pay the doctor? Or do we pay the plumber?"

Even while we asked the question, we realized that a number of more serious things could have happened. We thought of a husband who had just lost his job, of a friend with a sick parent and someone else with a critically hurt child.

Yet there are occasions when it doesn't help to know that someone else is in worse condition than we are. Too often problems seek us out when we are least prepared for them. Perhaps we have been up several nights with the baby, or someone we know just rubbed salt into our wounds by raving about their three-week vacation.

Furthermore, we would be able to handle one thing at a time, but when many difficulties occur at once we feel as if we're drowning. Our anger bubbles up, spilling over, as we ask ourselves, "Why did this have to happen? I just wanted to enjoy my baby right now."

Sometimes simply talking about the situation with someone gives us the sense of release we crave. But then we need to make an honest effort to put our feelings aside rather than indulging in self-pity.

When we are tempted to feel sorry for ourselves, it might help to imagine Christ standing before Pilate, his back laid open by a leaded whip, his temple bleeding from a crown of thorns. Bearing the weight of the entire world, he himself was blameless. If we keep that image in mind, it's much harder to become waterlogged with self-pity. Christ's image can help us believe that God will bring something good out of whatever problems we face.

As someone has said, "A grandfather clock does not work without weights. They provide the energy needed to push the hands ahead." Though none of us would choose to be afflicted with problems, they can prove to be the weights pushing us ahead—into learning to take one thing at a time, into a new level of growth in our spiritual lives.

A passage in Isaiah reminds us how God helped his people with their problems:

> Fear not, for I have redeemed you;
>   I have called you by name, you are mine.
> When you pass through the waters
>   I will be with you;
>   and through the rivers, they shall
>   not overwhelm you . . .
> For I am the Lord your God,
>   the Holy One of Israel, your Savior.
>
> Isa. 43:1-3

We might wonder how the Israelites felt while crossing the Red Sea. After an east wind blew all night, the people walked through on dry ground, a high wall of water on their left, a high wall on their right.

Moreover, they crossed the Jordan, not during a season of drought, but at flood stage. Only when the feet of the priests touched the water did it stop flowing. The water upriver piled into a heap, standing there as the children of Israel passed over.

In each case, it would have been easy to ask, "When's that water going to flow over us? When's it going to start running again?" But in faith they crossed over into a land of blessing.

"Fear not," said their Lord, as he says to us today. "Fear not. I have redeemed you. I have called you by name. You are mine."

One afternoon in July, my husband and I stretched out on lawn chairs near the shallow end of a motel swimming pool. Now and then water sprayed us as our attention centered on a brown-eyed girl of about five. Long hair flying, she flopped into the water, then stood up.

"Daddy, I want to jump off the diving board," we heard her say.

"But you don't know how to swim," he protested.

She looked up confidently into his eyes. "You catch me," she said.

Together they climbed out and strolled around the pool to the deep end. While the little girl walked onto the board, her father positioned himself close to where she would land. Then, squealing with laughter, she jumped into the water and the safety of his arms.

In each of our lives there are times when we fear drowning because of problems we face. Yet we can walk out on the diving board and jump confidently into life, secure in the knowledge that God wants to see us reach the edge of the pool.

That's the gift of our Father's arms around us, keeping us safe in deep water.

I'm discouraged, Lord,
and with good reason too.
Yet thanks for listening.
Thanks for saying, "Fear not;
I have called you by name, you are mine."

When I begin to feel sorry for myself,
help me remember your suffering.
Let me know that you are with me
whenever I'm swimming in deep water.
Thanks that you will bring me
safely to shore.

14

Just be Mary

Some weeks ago one of my friends had the courage to say, "Lois, when I look at you I see two persons. One is Mary, but the other is Martha, troubled about many things. Just be Mary. Let God's love flow over you."

During much of our lives we must be Martha, *taking care* of countless details. But we need not be the Martha who is *troubled* about many things, bound by concern or fear.

Sometimes our concern is for something happening now. Other times our fears involve something that might happen in the future. We stand beside the bassinet which holds our sleeping infant and wonder, "Into what kind of world did my child come?"

We hear friends talking about their teenage children and we ask ourselves, "What will my son or daughter be like at that age?" And then, "Will I be able to cope with whatever lies ahead?"

It's not hard to be that kind of Martha. All we have to do is jump two steps beyond tomorrow.

But what does it mean to be Mary? Perhaps it involves taking one moment, or however many moments are needed, to kneel at the feet of Jesus.

For some of us this means simply taking the time to kneel. In my case it meant even more. I began to realize that I was using my preoccupation with many things to avoid facing a difficult situation. Only when I envisioned myself sitting beside Christ's feet could I say, "Lord, here it is. Here's what's bothering me. I give you every detail, as well as my fears about the whole thing." Then I could sense once again that I am important to God just because I am me.

When we wrap a receiving blanket around our baby, we tuck that child into a cocoon of our love. Even so, the blanket of God's love covers us, promising us victory over any concern we might have now or in the months and years ahead.

As mothers, there may be moments when our joy is threaded by concern or even pain. Perhaps we knew that concern soon after birth as we watched our premature infant struggle to breathe and thrive. Perhaps we knew that pain as the doctors discovered a defect or if we had to wait before bringing our baby home.

Possibly we have yet to learn of that concern and pain. Perhaps it will come when another mother's remark forces us to see a comparison between our children, making us feel our child is inferior.

Whenever that moment arrives, we face the question we ask about any problem: Why? It is a question we must ask. But at some point we need to stop asking and start accepting. We need to say, "I can't understand this, Lord, but give me the grace to accept it. Give me the love to live with it. Give me the dignity to grow through this instead of becoming bitter."

Then healing can begin. We remember to look up into the face of Jesus, accepting the promise Paul gave us: "Our fears for today, our worries about tomorrow, or where we are—high above the sky, or in the deepest ocean—nothing will ever be able to separate us from the love of God demonstrated by our Lord Jesus Christ when he died for us" (Rom. 8:38-39 LB).

The rain falls on the just and the unjust, we are told. We are heirs of the lot common to all. Yet Christians are promised greater resources for facing hurt and concern. As we sit at the feet of Christ, we see not only his love, but also the power he wants to give us.

Can any of us fully realize the scope of that providing? Paul writes: "I pray that you will begin to understand how incredibly great his power is to help those who believe him. It is that same mighty power that raised Christ from the dead and seated him in the place of honor at God's right hand in heaven" (Eph. 1:19-20 LB).

Resurrection power! And all Christians have access to it. But if we are to live by that power both now and in the future, we need to evaluate our thinking regarding Christ as Savior.

If we believe that Christ's death was God's provision for taking care of our sinfulness, we are able to confess whatever sin the Holy Spirit calls to our attention. This includes, whether we like it or not, any fear which binds us, for as someone has said, "Worry is praying to the wrong god."

We can admit to God our difficulty in trusting his ability to care for us. Then we are ready to yield ourselves completely to him—yielding not only surface concerns but also our innermost beings.

Sometimes that yielding is difficult. Because God formed us with free wills, he will not violate that creation. He will not rob us of our gift of choice.

That means each of us needs to trust him enough to say, "Lord, I know you have great things planned for me. I don't have to be bound by worry or fear. Here's the situation. I'm turning it over to you."

In essence we are telling him, "I believe your will for me involves the very best. I want my will to be at one with yours."

To the degree that we surrender our wills to God, he is able to work in us. For if we have yielded, we can pray, "Lord, I need your power in my life. I know you have promised to give the power of your Spirit to every person who asks. I ask for the fullness of that power."

God keeps his promises. All we have to do is believe that because we have asked, the Spirit's power is working in every aspect of our lives. With a trusting heart we can say, "Thank you, Lord, for what you are going to do."

One evening when our oldest son was 10, I walked into his bedroom. He was already asleep, sprawled across the bed, fully clothed. Both arms were up, his hands clasped, forming a cradle under his head. His white-blond hair escaped from beneath the red baseball cap he still wore.

The dirt of the day smudged his cheeks, but a half-smile curved his lips. And across his closed eyelids drifted the softness of peace.

No matter what the smudges of our day are, no matter what the future holds, we don't need to be Martha, troubled about many things. We can let God's love, his power, and his peace flow over us, blanketing us completely.

We are just being Mary.

Remind me, Lord,
whenever I am troubled about many things,
to simply be like Mary,
trusting you completely.

I give you each of my concerns,
each reason for pain.

Help me yield myself to you.
Flow over me and into me.
Control me. Possess me.
Thank you for sending
your Spirit's power
into my life.

15

Who will
be the mom?

Our two sons had received woodburning sets for Christmas. Now, as the icy fingers of winter clutched the corners of our house, they sat at the kitchen table, pressing brown imprints into wood.

"The tip keeps falling off," complained the youngest.

For the fifth time I picked up the pliers, tightened the tip, and returned the woodburner to him. "I wish I were a kid again," I said, trying to encourage him. "Then I could do all these fun things."

Our nine-year-old looked up from the design he was creating. "But then who would we have for a mom?"

Ah-ha! Who would be the mom? Sometimes I wondered myself. In his mind was my role synonymous only with work?

Then I realized that my son's question was also an admission of his need. It seems that for us mothers, our being needed and the work we must do as a result are inseparable. Perhaps the only alternative is the abyss of loneliness.

Yet if we have older children as well as an infant, we sometimes feel the demands upon us are overwhelming.

"When I had only one child I was used to being on the go," one person remarked after the birth of her second. "Usually it was for a good reason. But at times I really resent my baby's schedule."

We may also feel that the things we enjoy are gone forever. One mother shared her frustration with a group gathered for coffee: "I cried last night," she said. "I thought about how much I like to golf, and I've only been once this summer. And I started wondering if I'd ever go camping again."

Yes, we are needed. Certainly, being a mother means hard work. We long for the day when our baby is old enough to give us more freedom. With a part of our inner selves we admit, "I'm frustrated and angry from being tied down."

But there's a further complication. As one mother said, "We had waited a long time for our first child. I wanted him very much. Yet one night when he was only two weeks old, I had just fallen asleep when he started crying. Immediately I resented him. 'Why can't he let me sleep?' I thought. And then I felt guilty about being resentful."

In many cases a sense of guilt is good because it reminds us of the difference between right and wrong. Yet at other times, as in this case, it is potentially harmful, for it keeps us from admitting a very honest need in our own lives.

In her classic *Children and Books,* May Hill Arbuthnot discusses seven basic needs of human beings. Among them is the need for change. She writes:

> Escape is reprehensible if it means a cowardly run-ning away from responsibilities or an unwillingness to face reality, but escape becomes a sensible measure of safety when it means pausing to catch our breath during a hard climb, or beating a hasty retreat before an onrushing truck.

As mothers, we are not exempt from the need to catch our breath or to escape from the traffic seeming to bear down upon us. One of my friends has two young children—a sixteen-month-old girl and a three-month-old boy. Yet with the encouragement of her husband, she is taking a history course at a nearby college and singing weekly with a small group.

She and her husband have caught the secret of a happy balance—a balance that enables her to return home, saying with enthusiasm, "I'm convinced that being the mother of two babies is an art. The more I put into it, the more satisfying it is."

John Mason Brown has told us, "Existence is a strange bargain. Life owes us little; we owe it everything. The only true happiness comes from squandering ourselves for a purpose."

Yet how can we reach that seemingly impossible feeling of satisfaction? Perhaps Solomon's words will help us.

"There is a time for everything," he says in Ecclesiastes. Then he asks, "What does one really get from hard work?" Answering his own question, he repeats, "Everything is appropriate in its own time. But though God has planted eternity in the hearts of men, even so, man cannot see the whole scope of God's work from beginning to end" (Eccles. 3:9, 11 LB).

We cannot see the whole scope of God's work. At

times it's hard to remember that we will be able to golf and camp once again—perhaps with that son or daughter who now is tying us down.

In Isaiah God tells us, "I have created you and cared for you since you were born. I will be your God through all your lifetime, yes, even when your hair is white with age. I made you and I will care for you. I will carry you along and be your Savior" (Isa. 46:3-4 LB).

That caring for us means opening the way for change when we need it. It also means that if we ask, he will plant a sense of eternity in our hearts to help us see the ongoing quality of the years. Awareness of that quality makes it easier to find satisfaction in providing whatever is needed in our children's lives.

Many years ago missionary Jim Elliot and his future wife Elisabeth were separated by thousands of miles. Each of them wanted to make the days pass quickly so they could be together as husband and wife. Yet out of the experience Jim wrote, "Let not our longing slay the appetite of our living."

In our role as mothers we may long for the time when our babies are older. Yet we don't need to wish away our lives. Though we seldom receive dramatic ovations or rounds of applause, we can cherish the present with an appetite for living.

We'll find the thanks for our long hours in quiet ways—in the feel of a small head resting on our shoulder, in the delight of seeing our baby strong enough to roll over, in the pleasure of singing our child to sleep.

As one new mother remarked, "I can change a lot of

diapers in exchange for one gurgle of response from
my baby."

Our ability to respond with joy to the needs of others
depends on having our own needs satisfied. For then
if we are asked, "Who will be the mom?" we can
answer with assurance, "*I* will!"

Yes, Lord,
I'm tired of working hard,
frustrated from being tied down.
I'd like to escape just for a day or two,
sit in long grass
with spring sunshine warm upon my back
and the wind tugging at my hair.

Yet use my need for change
to instill in me
a sense of thankfulness
for the daily changes in my baby.
Work through my child today
to show me your love.
Let my child's need of me
plant a sense of eternity
in my heart.

16

Mount up with wings

"At first after the baby was born I felt weak and tired, and was thankful for each day I was stronger," remarked one mother. "But now the baby is sleeping through the night and I'm still tired. It's emotional, I guess, instead of physical. But what's so beautiful about motherhood?"

About that time we catch a glimpse of ourselves in the mirror. Our question comes even closer to home: "My stomach is flabby. My hair is scraggly. What's so beautiful about *me?*"

If we long for a sense of beauty, we may need a change. Yet it isn't always possible to escape the everyday-ness of our lives. In weary moments it might help to consider the words of Isaiah: "They who wait for the Lord shall renew their strength, they shall mount up with wings like eagles, they shall run and not be weary, they shall walk and not faint" (Isa. 40:31).

We wonder, how would it feel to run without weariness, to walk long distances without feeling faint? If we have a baby resting on one hip and a toddler hanging onto our hand, it takes concentration just to cross the street. If we leave for overnight, it seems as if we're carrying along the entire house. It's hard to imagine mounting up with wings.

But what does it mean to soar as freely as an eagle? How do we wait for the Lord, renewing our strength?

Sometimes waiting for the Lord involves acceptance of circumstances in which he has placed us—acceptance, and willingness to see the beautiful within those circumstances. As we learn to see the beautiful, we sense a renewal in our strength, for we aren't wasting needless energy on might-have-beens.

Ability to see the beautiful does not come to any of us overnight. Yet it's a quality all of us can develop. Often it helps to consciously create beauty in areas where we do much of our work.

During the years our two youngest were active preschoolers, my husband initiated that creation. When the winds of February howled outside, he'd bring home a small pot filled with crocus bulbs ready to bloom. I'd set those bulbs on the kitchen table where I could see them often.

I knew that without words he was saying, "Watch the buds open one by one. Believe that spring *is* coming soon. And incidentally, I love you."

Since that beginning, I've created many spots that mean something to me. I've placed rocks we've collected on the window ledge above the kitchen sink. Nearby I've hung favorite plaques, often mind-joggers such as the one which says, "The Lord respects me when I work, but he loves me when I sing."

Recently I made use of the short section of cupboards between our refrigerator and built-in oven. Beneath the top cupboard and the counter I hung a five-by-seven oil painting. Not an expensive one, but a painting that gives me the feel of warm sand, rushes bending in the wind, seagulls soaring and waves lapping.

One son said, "That's a strange place to hang a picture, Mom. No one will ever see it." But I do. Many times a day I see that painting.

To see the beautiful in everyday circumstances, we need to consciously create an oasis in which to renew our strength. No matter how busy we are, we should take at least 15 minutes during the day or evening to do whatever we like best.

Each of us may choose a different activity. If exercise is our thing (or our need), we can do something physical. If doing our hair or polishing our nails makes us feel better, that's great. Or we may want to read, listen to records, paint, knit, or do needlepoint.

One mother of three, who also carries a full-time teaching load, said to me: "I'm a very private person. I need moments when I'm by myself. I need to do enough thinking to be rejuvenated."

Other mothers, who don't work outside the home, feel just the opposite. "I need to be with people," said one.

However we use our oasis, it should provide a time of affirmation. We hear much about the importance of positive thought patterns. We need to feed "I enjoy" thoughts into the computer that is our subconscious. "I enjoy being a mother," for instance. Yet secular affirmation techniques fall short unless coupled with a resource outside ourselves.

If we wish to see the beautiful, mounting up with wings above daily circumstances, we need the quality of inner beauty. Peter said, "Be beautiful inside, in your hearts, with the lasting charm of a gentle and quiet spirit which is so precious to God" (1 Peter 3:4 LB).

This charm comes from learning to wait upon the Lord, from learning to rest in him, believing that he is in control.

In longing to mount up with wings, we often make the mistake of trying to find our satisfaction in circumstances or in people. We expect too much of those around us. We think that if we could change this or that we would be happy.

It is easy to chase an illusion, believing that life must always be exciting or romantic. In doing so, we haven't yet learned to live with necessary everyday-ness.

We can soar as an eagle when we allow God to use whatever situation we're in to create something beautiful *within us.* The joy he gives lasts in spite of circumstances. As Teilhard de Chardin has said, "Joy is the most infallible sign of the presence of God."

After coming from a Bible study on Galatians 5:22, a mother of two small children said, "I need that love, joy, peace, patience, and self-control we talked about. I could use it every day at home."

Those qualities of inner beauty become available as we understand the difference between God's work in salvation and his work in our spiritual growth. As one pastor explained: "With salvation we *accept*—it's a free gift. But if we want the fruit of the Spirit to grow in us, we *cooperate.*"

That means we don't have to work frantically to be patient, loving, or full of joy. But we do have to learn to cooperate, remembering that God precedes us. His act goes before ours in every fruit and work.

The key to living with new emotions lies in the words, "But when the Holy Spirit controls our lives he will produce this kind of fruit in us" (Gal. 5:22 LB).

As Christians, we have the Spirit dwelling within us, yet we don't always allow him to have all of us. Allowing him to produce fruit is not always easy. Sometimes it involves pruning, and that hurts. Yet we may learn more about patience by living with a fussy baby than we would any other way. And that's what inner beauty is all about.

But that's not very exciting, is it? By contrast we often hear of women who are celebrities or whose jobs take them throughout the country or the world. Sounds terrific, doesn't it? Maybe it is at first, before the routine sets in for them too.

Yet those of us with inner beauty can mount up with another kind of wings, those of the Spirit.

At a meeting for church school teachers, we were asked, "What do you feel is the most beautiful thing on this earth?" A public school bus driver spoke up. "For me, it's the expression in the eyes of a little kindergarten girl. It's the smile she has when she climbs aboard, looks up, and sees that I'm there."

In our arms we hold a child who can give us that same smile, looking up and seeing we are there.

Lord, I long to soar as an eagle,
not always searching for happiness
in other places or other people,
but mounting up
because you have given me that ability.

Help me to cooperate,
allowing you to produce
the love, the joy, the peace, the patience—
all I need for daily life.

Create in me the inner beauty
that lasts in spite of circumstances.
Give me wings, Lord.
Wings.

17

Better than
a grandmother

"Let me take care of your boys when they're ill," said an elderly woman to one of my friends.

Strange request, I thought. That's the *worst* time to have small children. Why would she want them then?

Her daughter-in-law wondered the same. "I'd love to, Grandma," she replied. "But won't you get too tired?"

The older woman smiled. "No," she said gently. "It's the only time my grandsons sit still long enough for me to hold them."

For some years I envied my friend having a mother-in-law who lived near by, able to say those words. My feeling about sickness contrasted sharply with the grandmother's attitude.

I thought of the tight knot in my stomach as I rocked an infant limp with fever, the ache between my shoulder blades as I paced the floor, jiggling a small body up and down. I remembered my weariness, my yearning to stretch out between smooth sheets with no plaintive toddler calling, "Mommy! Mommy!"

Was holding a baby or small child really worth the dragged-out feeling left by sleepless nights?

I still dislike illness, especially when it comes to someone I love. But gradually I came to understand that I have a resource even better than a grandmother, not in human form but divine.

I began to realize that I needed to live my understanding of Paul's words, "My grace is sufficient for you, for my power is made perfect in weakness" (2 Cor. 12:9).

What might that weakness involve? When our children are ill, it may be fear of what will happen. It may be exhaustion from lack of sleep. It may be worry about whether we're doing the right thing.

But when we are aware of our weakness, we begin to comprehend the immensity of God's power, a resource we often neglect. He offers many channels through which to receive that power. He wants us to use, not only the medical people he has provided for us, but also the resource of prayer. James offers a promise:

> Is anyone sick? He should call for the elders of the church and they should pray over him and pour a little oil upon him, calling on the Lord to heal him. And their prayer, if offered in faith, will heal him, for the Lord will make him well; and if his sickness was caused by some sin, the Lord will forgive him (James 5:14-15 LB).

In a letter to a pastor, Martin Luther discussed these verses in detail, telling how to make practical application of them. Bengt R. Hoffman, in his book *Luther and the Mystics,* explains:

There is among Luther's letters a document which shows us beyond any doubt that he viewed spiritual healing as an integral part of the pastoral task of the church. He did not forget that medically trained people should be consulted. But especially when their counsels seemed at an end the constant necessity for intercessory prayer stood out plainly.

Those of us belonging to a sacramental church can also avail ourselves of the opportunity offered in the Lord's Supper. When we take Communion, we meet Christ in a very real and personal way. As we go forward to receive the bread and wine, we can bring our children along for the blessing. We can ask for our healing or for theirs. In some churches pastors use this occasion to pray with the laying on of hands for those with illness.

If our child is ill, we can seek prayer help from our pastor and the leaders of our church. More often, however, we are concerned about our child but don't feel the illness is serious enough to call in someone else.

During those occasions we can pray for our children by ourselves or in agreement with our husband, combining our prayers with the scriptural laying on of hands. When Christ commissioned his disciples to go out into the world, he said, "And those who believe shall use my authority. . . . They will be able to place their hands on the sick and heal them" (Mark 16:17-18 LB).

When we hold a baby, it is very natural to cup a small head in our hands. As our children grow, we instinctively smooth their feverish foreheads. As we rock them, we rub their backs.

If we take James 5 seriously, we can combine these

92

everyday expressions of love with our petitions, giving God the opportunity to send his healing power through the touch of our hands. Our human love combines with his divine love.

As we pray, we remind ourselves, first, of God's presence within us by thanking him for it. Then we ask simply, "In the name of Jesus, I ask for the healing of my child. Thank you for what you are going to do. Amen."

By praying in the name of Christ we depend on his authority. Thanking him in advance offers our belief in his power. *Amen* adds the final "So be it."

If we seek God's healing, it is important that we ask in faith. Often it helps to use the method suggested by Agnes Sanford in *The Healing Light*—to visualize the person we are praying for in good health, or in her words, "to see him well."

But what about the times when our prayers aren't answered in the way we hope?

When we pray for physical healing, we realize there are circumstances in which the kingdom of God has not yet come perfectly upon this earth. As Christians, we believe that ultimate healing comes in the resurrection. We don't need to lose our faith because of the way the answer to prayer comes. While we seek physical wholeness, we understand that another kind of healing is even more important. That healing comes when the kingdom of God dwells within us or within our afflicted child.

I know people restricted to wheelchairs who feel they have received healing. When I am with them, I realize how important it is that we as mothers be whole persons so we can help our seriously ill or exceptional child.

It is my belief that the son of my friend Pat Rosenberg will be a whole person as he grows older because his mother has allowed God to develop spiritual wholeness in her. Her son Paul is confined to a wheelchair with cerebral palsy.

"Yes, I have days when I'm down," says Pat. "I wonder if I can go on. When Paul has some kind of illness in addition to the palsy he suffers from, I often stand by his bed, asking for the strength to keep going.

"People must simply despair if they don't believe or rely on God. I can't imagine life without him. I know he walks with me every day. I couldn't do it otherwise."

I wondered if she often faced the question most of us do about a difficult situation.

"Yes, I've asked, 'Why me, Lord?' " Pat answered. "I go through times of real questioning. I feel limited, for instance, in what I'm able to do because of Paul's condition. I get frustrated when people say, 'How do you manage?' There are times when I feel very much alone. When I ask, 'Does anyone know I have this problem?'

"But I always feel the good overshadows the bad," she continued. "I have a great deal of support from my husband, his family, and my family. I've made wonderful friends because of Paul. I don't think I would otherwise have chosen to be active in cerebral palsy work, and I feel I'm contributing in that area.

"I believe so strongly that the Lord has a plan for us. I believe that we must accept many of the things that come into our lives. It took me awhile to realize this. I didn't accept all these things overnight. But my faith has been strengthened because of having Paul."

Spiritual healing? Yes! Pat has found the resource better than a grandmother. And every day her son lives in the atmosphere of her wholeness.

When my child is sick,
it's so easy to be afraid, Lord,
and so hard to believe.
Remind me in those times of the resources
you offer to everyone who loves you.
Give me the strength, the wholeness I need.

Fill me with the ability to trust,
so that whether the healing my loved one receives
is physical or spiritual,
my faith in you will grow stronger.

18

A bus filled
with oranges

If our children are physically ill, it seems natural to
pray for them. If we need strength to take care of
them, we again turn to God for help. Yet there is an
additional resource we often forget. We can ask for
wholeness of spirit for our children.

Some time ago I had lunch with a charming boy
named Tommy, who would soon celebrate his third
birthday. With a wealth of brown hair and dark brown
eyes set above high cheek bones, Tommy is a beautiful
child physically.

Yet his spirit captivated me even more. Maintaining
continual chatter, Tommy devoured a large apple and
a small bag of Fritos, then downed a big glass of milk.
Next he attacked his orange, wanting to peel it himself. When he couldn't quite manage, I helped with
the remaining peeling.

Then Tommy took over again, pulling apart the
segments by himself. Spreading an oblong napkin on
the table, we made a bus filled with the segments.
Three pieces formed the driver. Individual segments

became passengers. Pulled by Tommy, the napkin "drove" around the tabletop. Then, one by one, he gobbled the passengers and, at last, the driver.

Watching Tommy, I would have guessed that he had enjoyed a protected infancy and a loving early childhood, but that was not the case. His adoptive father told me about Tommy's background and a special prayer we can give our children.

Coming out of a home where his mother left him alone all day, Tommy suffered from severe malnutrition. At 11 months, he was unable to lift his head. On his first birthday, when he was placed in a Christian foster home, he hadn't had even his DPT shots. From midchest to midthigh, he was covered with diaper rash that had turned into ulcerated sores.

Two months later, when Tommy came to his adoptive parents, the sores had healed, leaving countless strawberry marks that looked like smallpox scars. Although 14 months old, he had only four teeth. He didn't want to be hugged or held. Little noises woke him immediately, and often he'd cry for three hours straight regardless of his new mother's efforts to calm him. Hardest of all was the way he woke up screaming at any time of the night, as though he were having nightmares.

Sometimes adoptive children come to us with emotional scars. Biological children may also accumulate wounds in spite of our best efforts to offer them security and a sense of peace.

In some instances, an older child needs professional counseling. In other cases the discomfort of teething may cause a baby to be wakeful. Or the baby may need medical consultation for some reason. But there are also times when a wakeful, tension-filled pattern can be helped through prayer and understanding.

As we pray about our child's problem, we can ask God to make us aware of needs and fears. Has a TV show been frightening? Is there a neighborhood friend who's pushing everyone around? Does our child feel the pressure of keeping up with an older sibling or ahead of a younger one? Or are we parents tense ourselves—worried about money or about finishing professional training?

Even a very young child can react to a disturbance nearby. An infant senses tension when being held. A two-year-old may cry whenever a baby cries.

Time may take care of such problems, or we may be able to change factors surrounding the situation. But other cases involve just the normal wear and tear of everyday existence. Whenever children are present, one hundred variables become possible.

As mothers, we know how quickly we become strained when our children are restless and irritable. We become even more tense if the trouble starts when we're in the car. If the usual diversions aren't effective, the baby may fuss for 50 miles. Or if the baby is happy, our other children aren't. Then the disturbance is not only distracting. A safety factor is involved.

During such times I've discovered one prayer to be very effective, probably because it helps me first. I ask, "Lord, let your love flow through me and into each person in this car." Then I take a deep breath, letting the Spirit's power relax me as I continue to ask for more love, as I ask that my family *sense* that love, as I ask that my husband and each child *receive* that love.

Perhaps it sounds too easy. Yet Colossians 2:6 promises, "Just as you trusted Christ to save you, trust him, too, for each day's problems; live in vital union with him" (LB).

Those skeptical might give it a try, not only in the car but also at home, for love combined with prayer has been effective not just in my family. It also changed Tommy into a charming little boy.

Often his adoptive father rolled with him on the floor, giving Tommy touching, fun-filled love. At night both parents stood by his crib, praying over him before he slept, and sometimes while he was sleeping and didn't know they were there.

Together they prayed that no evil would hurt him, that he would sleep in peace, that the Holy Spirit would protect his mind from anything that would cause unrest. And from that love combined with prayer developed the happy, imaginative child who drove a busload of orange segments around the table.

Lord, I need your wisdom.
Guide me so I realize
when my child needs professional help,
but also create in me
an awareness for the times
when my child needs prayer and understanding.

Give me your discernment in knowing
when and how to pray.

Give my child the wholeness of spirit,
the sense of peace and love
that flows abundantly from you.

19

So you want to be you?

"I can see that babies are individuals even when they're just a few days old," remarked a pediatric nurse. "There's a difference in the way they eat. Some like to be held more than others. And some are fussy, others content."

An obstetric nurse agreed, telling of her experience with a three-pound, nine-ounce infant delivered by emergency cesarean section after a 34-week gestation.

"He was fed with a premie nipple every other feeding," she said. "He did so well that it wasn't necessary to transfer him to a larger hospital where he could receive intensive care."

The nurse found that the baby showed a remarkable will. "As the nurses cared for him, they turned him on his side with a diaper roll at his back," she said. "But he wasn't content to stay where he had been put. Even before he was two weeks old, he managed to move completely away from the diaper to the opposite end of the isolette."

As we live with our children, we realize how

quickly babies show their likes and dislikes, expressing individuality. We begin to understand how long a time we have had to develop our own individuality. To further complicate the situation, we see other women struggling for recognition and equality.

We realize very quickly that the way we feel about being a woman affects the way we feel about being a mother, which in turn influences the way we encourage our children to develop. It becomes necessary to ask, "How can I reconcile my identity as a person with my role as wife and mother?"

Most of us have probably already decided which issues in the liberation movement are meaningful to us. Certainly we can all sense the need to avoid damaging sexual stereotypes in children's literature. We would also advocate equal pay for equal work. So too would we agree on the importance of a woman having the opportunity to become as educated as she wishes to be and to go as far in her chosen profession as her abilities make possible.

Yet where does the dividing line between balance and imbalance come? We wonder, what is a legitimate need for justice and what is simply a selfish demand?

"It's strange," said one mother who works with a number of avowed liberationists. "They laugh at my suburban housewife syndrome. They feel that I'm bound by my loyalty to my family and by my desire to contribute all I can to their happiness."

Then she grinned. "But as I see it, those women are working as hard to fit their pattern of nonconformity as I work to conform to my family's needs. Instead of being released by their demands, they are bound by them."

There is a danger that vocal women may put others of us into a position where we really don't care to be. At times it takes courage to express our true feelings. As one young woman said, "I'm almost afraid to admit that I like being a mother. I enjoy being home with my baby. I want to make the most of my opportunity to guide the way she thinks and believes. Yet sometimes I'm made to feel as if I'm an unheard-of phenomenon."

If we are reluctant to tell others that we *do* enjoy being mothers (most days, that is!), our lack of honesty can bind us. In her best-selling book *Times to Remember,* Rose Kennedy speaks from her experience as mother of nine children:

> I now realize that I had a considerable part in form-ing the characters of our children. Naturally, I had very good material to work with. Yet I knew what I wanted from them. I didn't always succeed in all my aims, but it was never from lack of effort. I looked on child rearing not only as a work of love and duty but as a profession that was fully as interesting and challenging as any honorable profession in the world and one that demanded the best that I could bring to it.

Often we forget that every ability we have was given to us by God or developed from his original gifts. We also forget that our biblical heritage offers a broad range of expression to the wife and mother. In Prov-erbs 31 Solomon describes the qualities of a wife freed by God.

She does not hinder her husband, but helps him, he says. She gets up before dawn to prepare breakfast and plan the day's work. She watches for bargains yet also buys imported foods. She provides clothing for the

102

poor (a thrift shop!) and sews for her family, managing her household carefully.

Moreover, she is honored for her attention to her home. Her children bless her and her husband praises her, saying, "There are many fine women in the world, but you are the best of them all!"

It may surprise us to realize that as far back as Solomon's day, wives and mothers had many options concerning the directions their lives should take.

We may choose one direction by working at a job consistent with good family life. The decision to work or not to work outside the home is one each woman needs to make for herself.

"I wanted to be an individual," said one mother with a new baby. "Keeping on with my job was my way of expressing my individuality. But then I realized how quickly my child was growing. I cut down on my hours and started making myself take time to appreciate his littleness."

Another mother, who works full time, tries to create special moments in the evening and weekends for her preschoolers. "I don't take our hours together for granted," she said. "When I go to bed at night I ask myself, 'What did I do to build something into my children today?'"

Both these mothers are emphasizing their responsibility to contribute to the good of their families.

Yet the question of individual roles may need further clarification. We are aware of much misunderstanding about Paul's teaching concerning the submission of wives. Some would have us believe that we should *seemingly* submit to our husbands in order to actually manipulate them. Others wonder if we are to be spineless amoebas skittering around on a slide while our husband gazes down through the microscope.

In Genesis we are told that woman was created from man's flesh to be a companion, "a helper suited to his needs" (Gen. 2:18 LB). The words "companion" and "helper" imply an attitude of friendly cooperation, of willingness to work together.

The word "willing" is not just implied, but used directly by Paul when he says, "You wives must willingly obey your husbands in everything, just as the church obeys Christ" (Eph. 5:24 LB).

Many people forget the word "willing" because they are bothered by the word "obey." Yet if we look at the sentence in its larger context, we see that we are told to obey our husbands *as the church obeys Christ*.

If a church is acting in obedience to Christ, it is working to fulfill Christ's commands—to go into the world teaching and baptizing, to love one another, to treat a neighbor as we want to be treated. And if the church is functioning well, it is obeying Christ's commands out of a sense of grace, not of works, out of the knowledge of being loved by Christ.

Doesn't this image of a church picture its people in creative, loving response? Not in a position that is subservient or degrading?

I have come to believe that if I act toward my husband as the church acts toward Christ, I can hope to live in creative cooperation, simply because I love my husband and respond to his love for me.

Marriage is not a one-sided arrangement. To husbands Paul writes:

Show the same kind of love to your wives as Christ showed to the church when he died for her. . . . That is how husbands should treat their wives, loving them as parts of themselves. For since a man and wife are now one, a man is really doing himself a favor and loving himself when he loves his wife! (Eph. 5:25, 28 LB).

If this Christ-like love is present, how could a husband rule his home as an impossible tyrant? And how could a wife want anything *less* than to be led in the kind of love involving mutual give and take?

A relationship of this depth encourages both husband and wife to grow because it is based on respect for individual roles—a respect that *values* masculinity and femininity.

This attitude, valuing not only the sexuality of both husband and wife, but also their entire personhoods, is extremely important in the development of our children. If we want them to have balanced, healthy sexual lives, we ourselves need to set the pattern.

Throughout our married life God has been teaching me that my responsibility as wife includes asking, "Lord, use me for good in the life of my husband," or "Lord, use me for good in the lives of my children." Being able to say those prayers presupposes the yielding advocated by Paul: "Honor Christ by submitting to each other" (Eph. 5:21 LB).

If we are Christians, the right to be an individual, whether male or female, cannot be equated with the right to do whatever we want. All of the Christian walk is a yielding—not a grasping nor a demanding—simply a yielding to accept Christ's best for us. That yielding involves a willingness to be used by God.

When the angel Gabriel told Mary that she would

become the mother of Jesus, she responded in belief, recognizing it as a privilege. "I am the Lord's servant," she said, "and I am willing to do whatever he wants" (Luke 1:38 LB).

The opportunity to be wives and mothers is a privilege, a cause for celebration throughout our lives. Yet it is also a responsibility.

As individuals we can serve, in whatever way we know best, offering the fullest expression of our personalities. But as someone said, "We need to be big enough to be little enough to allow God to use us."

Thank you, God, for creating me as an individual.
Thank you that while you gave me the ability
to develop in many ways,
you also gave me guidelines
about my calling as wife and mother.

Help me see the joyous potential
of your plan for me.
Give me the wish
to be an exciting, fulfilled individual
within that plan.

Guide me in my relationships
with my husband and children
so that I am big enough
to be little enough
to allow you to use me.

20

I, too,
have a dream

"I have a dream," sang out Martin Luther King Jr. to the throngs gathered before the Lincoln Memorial.

"I have a dream," that resonant voice echoed around the world.

"I have a dream that my four little children will one day live in a nation where they will not be judged by the color of their skin but by the content of their character."

"I have a dream today."

I, too, have a dream. Doesn't each thoughtful parent?

But less than five years after speaking those words, Martin Luther King Jr. died for his dream.

As mothers, we hope to live for ours.

We hope to see our children live in freedom.

We hope to see them happily married.

We hope to see them living responsible, productive lives.

We hope to see their lives inspired and shaped by God.

In the early stages of our child's growth, we see the firsts—the first tooth, the first step, the first tumble, the first word. Because the child is ours, those firsts are milestones. And seeing each step, each milestone, we wonder, "What will my child be?"

A farmer who tills the earth, providing food for the hungry of the world?

A man or woman seeking to give spiritual nourishment for those with another hunger?

A teacher perhaps—one changing the future by caring about what a child learns through books or through life?

A person serving through a trade? Or involved in business, honest in small tasks and in large?

Or yet, someone who seeks to heal through medicine or through social work? Who seeks to change the vision of others through painting or sculpture, through literature or music, or through exploration of the unknown?

Or will my child build another way, through forestry or architecture, engineering or politics?

Yes, we can well ask, "How will my child's life be spent?" Or perhaps it would be better said, "How will my child's life be *given?*" In leading a great cause? Discovering a cure? Investing God-created talents in science, in the arts, in business, in humanity?

And, most important, will my child's life be centered around faith in a personal Lord?

Kate Douglas Wiggin has said, "Every child born into the world is a new incarnate thought of God, an ever fresh and radiant possibility."

If we could choose what our child would become, would we define it in terms of a slot to fill or rather in spiritual goals? Perhaps we need to ask, "What will my child know?"

Our first wish is for happiness. But would our child learn more from pain?

Our second thought is for outward appearance. But would our son or daughter discover greater heights if forced to develop from within?

Our third concern is for our child's well-being. But in what terms do we define ultimate success—in the ability to win in every situation? Or in our child's emotional and spiritual resources to cope with whatever life offers?

For what then can we hope? That we as mothers succeed by encouraging our children to become independent of us? That we love our children enough to allow them to become themselves? Is this the finale of the dream?

Too often we realize that the weakness within us could blind our vision of the dream. Our fear could keep us from allowing our children to grow into whole beings, redeemed and filled by Jesus Christ.

We need power to counteract our concern about what lies ahead—reliance on the promises of God, belief in the words Paul wrote to Timothy: "For the spirit that God gave us is no craven spirit, but one to inspire strength, love, and self-discipline" (2 Tim. 1:7 NEB).

God has given us a spirit that lives not in fear of the future but in reverence of God—a spirit that claims the promise of Psalm 25: "Where is the man who fears the Lord? God will teach him how to choose the best. He shall live within God's circle of blessing, and his children shall inherit the earth" (vv. 12-13 LB).

For God has given us a spirit that says, "Lord, as I give my child a name, I ask for your greater name within the family of God."

He has given us a spirit that says, "Even as Hannah brought her son to the temple, so I bring my child to you."

He has given us a spirit that realizes how large Hannah's act became because of the man of God that Samuel became—a spirit that prays yet today, "Lord, as Hannah gave, I give my child to you. May my child also become your person."

Yes, I have a dream. I want to live, not in fear of what will happen to my child, but within the circle of blessing. I want to live in the belief that my child is also God's child, supported and cared for by him in each moment that lies ahead.

I want to live in the accumulation of those moments, for in them I will form the habit of a lifetime of trust.

I want to see my child learn that same trust, experience that same Lord Jesus, know that same love.

Yes, I have a dream. And I want to see that dream become reality.

We have a dream, my husband and I—
a dream so big
that it's impossible without you.
We give our child to you
for the moments that are now
and for the moments that are to come.
Work in that life, Lord,
making our child yours.

Teach us to dwell
within your circle of blessing.

110

Give us the ability to instruct and guide.
Give us spirits that are freed
by our reliance upon you.
Help us to live so that our child
learns to trust,
wishing always to grow in experience of you.

Thank you, Lord, that in the years ahead
you will be with our family.
Thank you that you will make our dream
become reality.